FLOWER GARDENING

Hamlyn Practical Gardening Guides

FLOWER GARDENING

Sean McCann

HAMLYN

Published in 1989 by
The Hamlyn Publishing Group Limited
a division of the Octopus Publishing Group
Michelin House
81 Fulham Road
London SW3 6RB

© 1989 The Hamlyn Publishing Group Limited

ISBN 0 600 56476 2

Printed in Italy

CONTENTS

INTRODUCTION

By using just a small packet of annual seeds or cuttings donated by a friend you can create a spectacularly colourful garden, packed with a wide variety of plants, including drifts of daffodils in spring, dazzling begonias, scented roses, waves of gypsophila, and the sweetly scented, old-fashioned wallflower.

Such plants, and scores of others, are very easily raised, which is one of the reasons why they are all so popular. But not only are they a delight in themselves, they are also an excellent way of transforming even the drabbest patch of ground. What might currently be a garden more noted for heaps of builders' rubble or three years of neglect and weeds can, after the ground has been cleared, actively be seen to come alive and take shape. As the spring sun warms the soil, so new flower beds will eventually begin bristling with shoots, so that by mid summer your eye will be attracted first to one patch of colour, then to another group of plants, in such a way that your garden immediately seems larger, dramatically richer, and infinitely more interesting.

However, to get things right you have got to plan ahead. You may not achieve the best associations straight away. Few people, even the owners of the greatest gardens in the country, never have to make any changes. After all, a garden should mirror your own loves and favourite combinations of plants, so don't be afraid to experiment or to rearrange if the result does not please first time. Flower gardening is a continuing experiment, that is part of its fun.

One thing that people tend to forget when creating a new garden, or rethinking their existing one, is that once you have done your work you will immediately be able to survey a new, brilliantly colourful world. Remember that it will take a season or two for your new plants to fill the spaces you have left them. Try not to think of your garden as *the* flower garden, which will be filled with every conceivable plant. That just isn't possible, even in the largest gardens. However, if that sounds depressing, consider that it also means you will have to be highly thoughtful and creative. What is the best plant for that one patch of damp, shady ground?

Why not devote that whole side of the garden to plants with foliage in one particular shade of grey-green, perhaps leading to a cluster of white plants at the far end? Colour themes in a garden give a spectacular result.

The more you think about your garden, no matter what its size or situation, the more you'll be aware of the fantastic range of possibilities. Planning ahead isn't that different from establishing the colour scheme and look of a favourite room. It should be a delight to enter, and excitingly different from anything your friends have designed. Colourful, magical – a sign of your creativeness, and an unrivalled opportunity to explore the different kinds of beauty possessed by the many hundreds of different plants that can be grown in our climate.

Right: A dazzling display of marigolds (*Calendula*) formally edged with bedding plants. These include begonias, lobelia, pansies and calceolaria.

Opposite: The flower garden in a different mood; rhododendrons, honesty (*Lunaria*) and pale pink *Polygonum bistorta*, backed by fruit trees in blossom.

CREATING A FLOWER GARDEN

There is no doubt in my mind that gardens are for flowers of every kind, from crocus to chrysanthemum, from snowdrop to cyclamen, from rose to simple pansy. Whether they are bulbous, annual, perennial or herbaceous, shrub or tree – there should always be something to keep colour in our lives no matter how drab our surroundings may be. Flowers give us colour as well as a very special excitement and pleasure. Flowers are for everyone and everywhere, whether it be in a garden of a great country house or a small cottage, in a window box on a busy street, or just a tumbling mass of lobelia in a small pot outside a doorway – flowers bring joy. The wonderful thing about them is that they can be grown with just a little care and attention. Provided you give them food, water, light and air – and a little bit of love you will have the makings of a marvellous garden. You do not have to be an expert to have plants in flower the whole year through.

Window boxes provide you with a great opportunity to experiment. After all, when you consider that in effect they allow you to select your soil, and that you can place them in full light or partial shade, it immediately becomes clear that they provide a fine opportunity for growing a wide range of colourful plants from early spring right through to Christmas. By changing the plants once or twice a year it is possible to try out new exciting plant colour schemes to keep the neighbours in constant wonder. Remember, even during the winter months small evergreens such as spotted laurel and variegated ivies will provide interest. They also form an attractive background, for example, for winter-flowering pansies or a variety of spring bulbs.

Another advantage for the modern gardener is that buying plants today is so much easier than in the past. There are more varieties now on offer, and there are few excuses for failing to raise them successfully, provided you buy first-rate plants and prepare the soil thoroughly. If

Tradescantia virginiana, the common spiderwort, named in honor of John Tradescant.

Fuchsia owes its name to Dr Fuchs; this is the popular cultivar 'Mrs Popple'.

you want immediate results, and are prepared to pay for them, you can even create an instant garden, complete with shed, lawn, paths, patio, beds of flowers in full bloom, and trees, all within a few days – just think of the Chelsea Flower Show!

THE OLD AND THE NEW

It isn't just the ease of gardening that has made flower gardens so attractive, for plant breeders are continuously breaking through new barriers creating new types of flowers, new colours, hardier varieties of previously tender plants, and miniatures of just about everything. Yet while today's gardening catalogue may be a wonderland of plants and colour, remember that not everything in it is new – the old flowers are still there, particularly the old style hollyhocks, snapdragons, and the sweet pea with its unmistakeable fragrance. So don't get too distracted by the new kinds of plants that are proclaimed at the Chelsea Flower Show each year – the older plants are available and should always be considered.

They are also an excellent reminder of the exciting early years when the Europeans were introduced to new flowers. For example tradescantia (perhaps better known as spiderwort) took its name from John Tradescant (1570/5–1638) the famous plant explorer, and fuchsia owes its name to Dr L Fuchs (1501–1566), the German botanist and herbalist. Incidentally, other plants were named in different ways. The delphinium is from the Greek for 'dolphin'; dianthus is from the Greek word *dius*, meaning 'God', and *anthos* meaning 'flower'; and it's possible tulip may have come from the Turkish *tulnana*, meaning a 'turban'. The names of many other plants are concerned with ancient myths and legends.

One problem for the amateur gardener is that some plant names seem difficult and forbidding. If so, take comfort from the fact that most have common names, which we shall use wherever possible.

GARDEN PLANTS

Over a century ago William Robinson (1838–1935), the eminent and influential Irish gardener and garden writer, wrote that '. . . a flower garden should be a thing of varied life.' He also offered the following advice to gardeners: 'Choose some beautiful class of plants and select a place that will suit them, even as to their effect in the garden landscape.' In that comment Robinson gives the key to what should be the great attraction of a garden. The plants should not only be carefully chosen, but carefully arranged. So, if you want to hide an ugly view, select tall growing plants that will eventually banish that eyesore; and if you want to emphasize a part of the garden or create a vista, then again consider your plants as part of an architectural plan.

The gardener must learn to view the garden from those parts that are most commonly used. Pick out what you would like to see when standing there, checking whether light colours will be best, whether you need height, or whether a specimen plant will be a winner. Yet this is not so much design in the flower garden, as taking an artist's view to produce something that will resemble a good painting. But don't forget, it will always be a 'painting' that you can reject or modify if you are unhappy with it, moving the various elements around and incorporating new ones where appropriate.

Low growing plants in full flower. White arabis, aubrieta and polyanthus associate well together and provide plenty of colour throughout the spring.

FLOWER GARDENING

An annual border in summer with red salvias, begonias, tagetes, and lobelia. All can be raised from seed. The silver foliage of *Senecio cinerea* is an excellent foil to the hot colours of the flowers.

FIRST CONSIDERATIONS

The first problem facing the gardener is deciding which sort of plants are needed. Making this decision involves answering a whole series of questions.

Do you want a permanent display, or will you be happy with a temporary arrangement, which can be changed next year or even next month if it doesn't look attractive? Note that your plants will have to be arranged around and between larger, more expensive, and probably permanent elements such as shrubs and trees. They are the 'main frame' of the garden. So too are the hardy perennials, which die down each winter but produce strong new growth the following year. Incidentally, some annuals behave in the same way, self-seeding and reappearing the following year, although you should not depend on that happening all the time and with every type.

The next question is, do you want to make the garden easy to look after? If you do then your choice will lean towards those plants that need little maintenance but provide long-term colour – many trees and shrubs obviously come into this grouping, but not all of these will fill a garden with that rich a diversity of plant form.

Roses, however, are a group of shrubs that will provide a marvellous array of colours, and provide long-term blooming, but remember they will require some attention for the best results.

Herbaceous borders can be equally colourful. They require a thorough preparation of the soil and careful planting, but once established they will need only routine weeding and dividing every three or four years for a wonderful return. In other words, there is no answer which does not require some input from you. And the greater your care and attention, the better will be the result.

Next, you must establish what size and shape plants you require. The biggest mistake made by gardeners is to plant a hedge that will grow and grow, needing cutting twice a year at least. That same hedge can also be a disaster if planted at the back of a flower border, for its enormous appetite 'eats' up the plant nutrients long before the flowers have had a chance to benefit from them. Permanent features, such as hedges and trees, should therefore

Primulas and grape hyacinths (*Muscari*) provide interest in spring when the branches are bare.

be planted with great care, and in places where they will be easy to maintain by clipping and pruning.

SELECTING GARDEN FLOWERS

The flower garden should be an amalgam of several elements. First, there are hedges and shrubs, which should be carefully chosen and very carefully placed. Then come the bulbs, many of which can be left in the ground until they need lifting because of overcrowding. The perennials, such as the delightful primula, will live for years in the herbaceous border or the rock garden, while annuals are planted, flower and die all within one season. Fourth are plants such as the sweet pea, border carnation, dahlia, chrysanthemum and fuchsia, many of which have cult followings, turning people who bought them, perhaps out of curiosity, into fanatics. Finally there are the roses – no garden would be complete without their wonderful blooms which they provide from May to December.

There can be little doubt that the annu-

Helipterum roseum, also known as acroclinium.

Bells of Ireland (*Molucella laevis*) is excellent for drying.

White tulips and lush green foliage provide a soothing colour association. The variegated foliage of euonymus continues the theme.

als and biennials provide the gardener with the widest range of plants, colour and fragrances for the least amount of money, but they do require some effort when it comes to seed planting, pricking out, weeding, watering, and dead-heading. Yet for variety and colour they are well worth the effort, as is immediately obvious on seeing a garden filled with the ever tolerant candytuft (*Iberis*), the massed colour of busy Lizzies (*Impatiens*), and the showy gazania. The flowering period for most of these plants is from June to October.

Plant categories

The dividing line between annuals, half-hardy annuals and biennials is very fine. Basically, the half-hardy annuals can be sown outside in May for late flowering, but they may need to be planted under glass and then pricked out if needed earlier. Some annuals can also be treated this way, but most are better sown directly into the ground where they will be left to grow on. Biennials seeds are sown this year to provide flowering plants the next year.

Most of the bedding plants that are sold by the million every summer belong to these categories, and they all provide excellent material for extensive bedding schemes, brightening dull corners, adding spots of colour to the rockery, and filling gaps in more permanent beds or borders. Of course, they can be spectacularly successful in hanging baskets, tubs and window boxes. To get the best results from most of these flowers give them a sunny position, well-cultivated ground, and plenty of light and air.

Drying flowers

In addition to providing garden colour, many annuals and biennials also provide delightful flowers for home decoration. However, do not try to emulate those ladies in the old Victorian garden prints who took flower cuttings and then placed them into large flat baskets. Flowers should be placed in water immediately on being cut, while those with woody stems will survive much better if the stem is cut *under* the water to avoid any risk of air-locks which will result in early wilting.

Bedding plants, such as the helichrysum (often called the straw flower), acroclinium (its proper Latin name is *Helipterum*, and its common name the everlasting flower), and *Molucella* (known as bells of Ireland because of the large green, bell-like calyx) also provide flowers which are excellent for drying. For the best results, take cuttings just before the flowers open.

Annual and biennial varieties of these flowers are extremely useful when you are brightening up very small areas with summer colour. Patio tubs, hanging baskets and window boxes all benefit greatly from them, but no-one would ever devote an entire garden, or even large sections of it, to annuals or biennials because the colour spread would not be good enough. These plants should be regarded as wonderful *additions* to the flower garden, growing side by side with the huge range of perennials in either the border or rockery.

Perennials

The perennials give a sense of permanence and beauty to borders and rockeries, and can be landscaped, unlike annuals, which are passing beauties being the 'chorus' to the main 'players' in the garden. A well planted bed or border of perennials will last for years, requiring very little work yet providing a marvellous display. While most of the plants will die down in winter, others will withstand the cold leaving your garden not entirely devoid of leaf and colour.

The most sensible place to grow perennials is in the herbaceous and mixed borders where the majority of plants will flower year after year, only needing to be worked on when they become too big for their allotted place, and are possibly deteriorating. They should then be lifted and divided into several clumps, the new outside growth being used to ensure a future supply of colour.

The problem with perennials grown from seed is that they can be quite slow to start, which means that the herbaceous beds or borders take a couple of years to reach their full potential. For a more immediate effect buy the larger plants that are available. The other problem is that there is a bewildering range of these plants from which to choose – from the tiny ground-hugging plants, that are called alpines or rockery perennials, to those that grow 30 cm (1 ft) or more high and are classed as border perennials.

For the ordinary gardener these plants will be best used in a mixed border or, if the space is available, as an island bed where the plants can be seen from all sides. Although roses and other woody type plants make a successful mix, the perennials are at their best when used as groups rather than single specimens. If you later find there are unwelcome spaces between the taller plants, they can always be filled with various annuals.

Bulbs

In addition to annuals, roses, and other shrubby types, there is always a place in the flower garden for bulbs, whether they be planted as separate subjects or within the various beds and borders. Although the word 'bulb' has a precise horticultural meaning, this is often overlooked and most people also include it to mean corms, tubers and some rhizomes (fleshy stems that creep below the surface producing plants such as the iris) in this category.

There is an extraordinary range of bulbs, with few other plant categories being able to provide the same amount of colour all the year round. Those more discerning gardeners who look beyond the familiar yellow daffodil and bedding tulip for something more unusual will find an even wider, excellent selection of new varieties of iris, gladioli, narcissus and daffodils, and tulips. Once you have selected your bulbs, you will need a well-drained, humus-rich soil which is, after all, the perfect garden soil.

THE SOIL

Every garden, every bed, every border, even the smallest rockery, is only as good as its soil. Afterwards come the imagination, dedication, seeds and plants that will make your dreams come true. But for the time being unless the soil is right for your chosen plants, you can expect no help from nature.

Fortunately garden soil can be improved beyond recognition within a short period of time, though many gardeners mistakenly find this an awesome subject. Your first task is to decide whether a particular site is composed of good, bad or average soil?

Let us begin by looking at the ideal soil. It should be medium textured, with small and medium-sized particles containing few stones, the sort of soil that is generally called loam. It will be crumbly to the touch, and will drain well holding some water but not becoming waterlogged during heavy rains. It should also be high in organic material, have sufficient lime to stop any sign of sourness, and have sufficient plant nutrients to make sure that plants reach their full flowering potential. In other words, you will generally find good loam soil in a garden that has been cared for over a number of years. Most of this soil will be contained near the surface, the depth of which will vary from area to area – from 5 cm (2 in) to 60 cm (2 ft). This top-soil can be distinguished from the sub-soil by the fact that it looks more alive and fresh, whereas the sub-soil is generally a lighter (often sickly) colour and looks inert. The trick is never to mix the two – keep the top-soil to itself by placing it aside when you have to dig deeply. Replace it when the bottom layer has been dealt with.

However, not everyone can be blessed by the perfect soil, so most gardeners have to work at improving their plots. The basic types of soil that will be encountered are:

Chalk soils
They have a white chalk (lime) sub-soil. The main problem is that since the land generally drains very quickly it needs generous amounts of manure and/ or compost to be dug in. And because of the quick drainage there is frequent leaching of the soil, which means that extra general fertilizer should be added, as well as iron and manganese, which will probably be needed once a year.

Clay soils
These are cold, wet and heavy in the winter, and therefore of little use for early crops. But if you are a rose grower you will see a lot of value in clay although you still need to add compost, moss peat, or stable manure to improve the texture and open up the solidly packed soil and allow it to be become aerated. Worked well with lots of organic material, especially moss peat, the clay soil can become much sought after loam.

Peat soils
These speak for themselves, being spongy and darkish grey or brown, and will be a delight for the grower of azaleas, rhododendrons and heathers. If you want to grow additional plants then you will have to investigate just how much liming is necessary to make the soil acceptable. While peaty soil can be very acidic and drains poorly, it is usually very fertile for adaptable plants.

Sandy soils
Another quick draining soil, being gritty and fast drying so that again a lot of compost, moss peat and organic material is required to improve its condition.

Stony soils
The back breaker – if you attempt to remove the stones! But once you realize that you will never achieve this without a complete transference of new soil to the site, you need only remove the larger stones for a well aerated and reasonably productive garden.

WEEDS AND OTHER GROWTH

These will also be a good indicator of the type of soil present – moss or a green slimy surface indicates that the drainage is bad; docks, buttercups or heathers usually reveal that it is an acid soil suitable for any plants that are listed later in this book. Good clover cover is an indication of alkaline soil, which means you will have problems growing good heather or azaleas. And, even though you will not welcome their presence, chickweed, nettles and groundsel indicate a productive, fertile soil. If you still require assistance in evaluating your soil type you can buy an inexpensive soil testing kit that will provide immediate answers. If you want even

Azaleas, here backed by *Magnolia x soulangiana*, flourish in a lime-free soil rich in peat.

more accurate help, approach a local gardening club where you will find information and help always at hand, or from a trained horticulturist.

The gardener who works with his soil and not against it is the one who will have most success, and who will get far more enjoyment from his garden. The main point to consider is that each type of soil is good for certain plants, so concentrate on growing them. First you must establish what soil is in your garden, or your new roses will not grow to their full potential, and your heather bed will be a source of dreams, not real enjoyment.

DRAINAGE, WATERING, AND FEEDING

Drainage is also a very important aspect of good gardening. Even if you have a moist, soggy garden which cannot be improved do not despair because there are many exciting plants that you can grow. Chinese loosestrife (*Lysimachia clethroides*) bears long spikes of tiny white flowers almost like a buddleia; the marsh marigold (*Caltha palustris* 'Flore Pleno') with its spring flowering golden heads can only survive in these moist conditions, while the hybrid astilbes with their long feathery plumes will be wasted anywhere else. However, in the well-drained garden your choice will never be restricted – the lists of flowers that will do well in these conditions would fill a book on their own.

Making the soil fertile by drainage, compost and/or fertilizer is the gardener's main responsibility. If you remember that soils can be upset and unbalanced by cultivation, it is obvious that a little help will be needed to restore things to their normal condition. This can be done by replacing three major soil losses, nitrogen, phosphorus and potassium, on a regular and well-planned schedule. When you have decided on your fertilizer read the instructions and use accordingly. You will soon be able to spot those gardens and plants that are undernourished. However, the real gardener does not wait for these signs but sets out with a calendar for feeding right through the year.

Most long-lasting flowers or plants will need some help at least once a month during their growing season (my own plan is to nominate the last day of every month

The double marsh marigold (*Caltha palustris* 'Flore Pleno') needs a permanently moist soil. It thrives in the shallow margins of a pool.

as feeding day). Fertilizing large areas is much easier than tackling small patches when the fertilizer must be kept off the plants lest it scorches the foliage. The way to ensure this does not happen is to measure out the quantity as recommended by the maker and put it into a small container. A matchbox may be ideal, but an old salt shaker is also very handy for distributing fertilizer among plants (make sure that from now on you restrict that salt shaker to the gardening box). Treat the ground around the plants uniformly.

However, feeding is not the main guarantor of success. Watering is just as vital being far more important than we imagine in these often wet summers. Some plants, such as roses and fuchsias, if growing on fairly well-drained land still need prodigious amounts of water and should never be allowed to dry out. Mature roses on a well-drained site will take up to 9.1 litre (2 gl) of water a day. Of course you don't have to molly-coddle them to that extent, but by watering them more frequently than most of us do they will be far healthier.

To ensure that plants get well watered and fed it is a good idea to use liquid or soluble fertilizers applied through a watering can or hose-end diluter. Liquid fertilizers are the answer where a quick result is needed because the necessary nutrients are immediately available to the plant. If you are watering frequently, increase the dilution by half or more. There is nothing that will rival a well-maintained garden, whose plants have been fed and watered regularly.

A diluter, easily attached to a hose end, will combine watering and feeding.

PLANTS FROM SEEDS AND CUTTINGS

You do not need to be an expert to raise plants from seeds. If you stop and think about it this is exactly the way the plants do it themselves, and if left to their own devices many would propagate without any help from the gardener. In addition, most perennials produce their own new plantlets each year, while daffodils and other bulbs will increase, if left undisturbed for a number of years, even though the increase in quantity can mean a decrease in quality.

However, this does not mean that when you have bought packets of seeds of annuals, half annuals or biennials, you can sow and forget about them. They will require some basic attention, but once they have been given moisture, oxygen, a reasonably high temperature and, eventually, a food supply, they will develop without any problems. Another bonus of sowing seeds is that this is an inexpensive way of providing new flowers every year, while providing the extra thrill of knowing that the plants are entirely your own work.

These plants traditionally raised from seed not only provide a good display in the garden but also a supply of flowers for cutting and drying. Note too, that seeds of half-hardy annuals, annuals and biennials must be treated in different ways.

HALF-HARDY ANNUALS

These are probably the most expensive types of seed to raise because they often need more care than annuals. Most would have originally come from the tropics and therefore cannot be planted out until the prospect of frost is over. They should also be raised under cover. The technique for planting them applies to many annuals that are to be planted out in heavy, wet, cold ground, and for some that are needed for early flowering.

The time to plant is generally in spring from March to April, and has to be done under the protection of glass, which may be an outside cold frame, a greenhouse, or even a sunny windowsill. The seeds not only need protection from frost but also a high temperature to start them growing.

The seeds can be planted in almost any clean container – a seed tray, seed pan or ordinary shallow flower pot will suffice. Whatever you use, do make sure that there are holes or cracks in the container for the water to drain away, and pebbles or stones in the compost to ensure the water drains away quickly. There are many seed composts available, the peat based ones generally being favoured because they are lighter to handle and provide good germination.

Firm the compost into the container with your fists or a small piece of board. At this stage the compost should be moist but not wet. Scatter the seeds thinly and then cover them with a very fine layer of compost. You will soon discover that there are many different types of seeds and that they need slightly different sowing methods. For instance, very fine seeds do not need to be covered at all – when handling them be sure that they do not stick to the firming board. (A good guide is to sow at twice the diameter of the size of the seed.)

Once you have sown your seeds you will need to cover the tray with a sheet of glass and put some dark brown paper or layers of newspaper on top. Keep the seeds warm, at a steady 16°C (60°F) to 21°C (70°F), and wipe and turn the glass daily.

SEED SOWING

1. Fill the tray with seed compost, firming lightly. Do not over compact.

2. Sow seeds thinly and, if necessary, sieve some fine sand covering on top.

3. Cover to keep out the light until the seeds germinate.

Once the seeds have started to germinate the seedlings will need light, so take away the paper, and prop up the glass at one end allowing in air. After a couple of days it can be removed altogether. The tray should also be gradually moved into full light, while the compost must be kept moist (but not wet).

PRICKING OUT SEEDLINGS

Lift seedlings using a dibber. Transfer to trays of potting compost and gently firm in.

When the first true leaves have developed you can prick out the seedlings and place them in other containers filled with potting compost. Lift the seedlings gently by the leaves, and not by the stems which can be very easily damaged. The young plants should be given room to develop and left in the shade until they have settled into their new containers.

The next stage involves hardening them off. The container should be moved to a cooler room or a garden frame where the seedlings can gradually acclimatize to the outside temperature. Later, transfer them outdoors for a few hours during daylight. And finally, one week before you need to plant them out, leave the seedlings outdoors all the time.

While such instructions might seem complicated and fussy, raising seeds is actually an enormously simple task. Nor should you be worried if you do not have a greenhouse or cold frame, for a windowsill is a perfectly acceptable substitute. However, when raising seeds in this way slightly after your technique. Sow the seeds in a container and then cover with a transparent polythene bag which can be fixed round the pot with a rubber band, and supported above the compost by a section of wire coat hanger bent into a loop, the two ends sticking into the soil. Keep the pot in a shady part of the window until the seedlings begin to appear. The plastic covering can then be removed. Again, make sure that the compost is kept moist but never soaking wet. Using this technique your seedlings will develop on the windowsill with as much vigour as those in the greenhouse.

Some of the most interesting half-hardy annuals include:

Ageratum (floss flower) Neat, powder puff heads, free flowering and long lasting. Needs lots of water. Keep sheltered if possible. Best known for its blue flowers, but there are other colours worth considering.

Amaranthus (love-lies-bleeding) Long tassles of tiny booms. Not all are red, there is also a *A. viridis* which carries green tassles. Thrives in full sun and does not need a very rich soil.

Antirrhinum (snapdragon) The old-fashioned snapdragon is *A. majus*, but there are many different types now available both in shape, range of colour (reds, yellows and pinks) and height. Often troubled by rust (for remedy, see page 92). It likes a well-drained, medium soil in a sunny position.

Arctotis (African daisy) Long stemmed, showy flower in all shades of yellow and orange which closes in the evening. Full sun, no soil preferences. Pinch out to encourage bushiness. Needs support. Remove the dead flower heads.

Calceolaria (slipper flower) The bedding calceolaria, as opposed to the larger version sold as a pot plant, is an old-fashioned, almost forgotten flower available in various colours. It is very good for growing in pots, tubs or window boxes. Enjoys full sun.

Celosia (cock's comb) A tender, delightful plant with plumes or crested heads in brilliant shades of red, yellow and orange. Lightish soil in a warm, sunny position is best. Excellent for cutting.

Cleome (spider plant) Scented with an exotic flower that resembles a spider or fisherman's fly. Comes in shades of pink and mauve. Needs good soil and a sunny position. Grows to 90 cm–1.2 m (3–4 ft).

It is easy to see how *Cleome spinosa* acquired its familiar name of spider plant.

FLOWER GARDENING

Cosmos (cosmea) Has fern-like foliage, flowers like single dahlias in white, crimson and all shades of pink. Good for cutting and for long-lasting garden display for which it should be dead-headed regularly. May need staking. Light soil, sunny spot.

Gazania (treasure flower) For the front of a bed, border or rockery. Daisy-like, showy, and a tendency to sprawl. The gold, bronze or apricot flowers close in the evenings. Sunny spot, light soil. Good for seaside gardens.

Heliotropium (heliotrope or cherry pie) An old flower retained for its heavy fragrance. Blooms are tiny. Must have a sunny spot and good soil. Look for the dark blue and purple cultivars.

Impatiens (busy Lizzie) Grows anywhere, and not just as a summer house plant. Can be grown in a shady, damp spot in the garden, but will also succeed in a dappled or sunny position. Available in a wide range of colours.

Limonium (statice or sea lavender) One of the everlasting flowers. Tiny, papery petalled flowers in every colour. Needs a light soil, sunny spot.

Lobelia One of the favourite edging plants. The royal blue variety is widely available, but it also comes in other colours, pale blue and carmine. Needs a rich, moist soil, and can grow well in shade.

Mesembryanthemum (Livingstone daisy) When it is given a light soil and full sun it will spread marvellously, almost flat on the ground. In less than full sun it will not do so well.

Mimulus (monkey flower) If you want a plant for a damp, shady spot, this is it. Available in orange, yellow and red, though there are also mixed colour cultivars. Must not be allowed to dry out.

Nemesia Multicoloured, easy to grow and quick to flower. Give it a sunny spot, lime-free soil is best; pinch out for bushiness and don't let it dry out. Cut back for a second bloom.

Nicotiana (tobacco plant) Grown for its fragrance. Modern cultivars produce the best flowers in shades of crimson, pink, purple, 'lime green' and white. Well-drained land with sun or dappled shade.

Petunia Among the most colourful (reds, pinks, mauves, yellow, white and bicolors) and dazzling plants for a sunny site, ideal for window boxes, tubs or hanging baskets. They will be very unhappy in prolonged wet or windy conditions. However, the Resisto strain will stand up to the rain.

Phlox Another plant that needs full sun if its tightly packed flower heads are to be seen to perfection. Great variety of colours – one of the best collections is 'Beauty Mixed' which includes white and shades of violet, pink and scarlet. 'Twinkle Star' is also a good choice. For rock garden, bed, window box. Beware of slugs.

Portulaca (sun plant) One of the half-hardies that do not like root disturbance. Plant outdoors where it will flower in a sunny and sandy spot. The blooms close up on dull days. They come in a wide range of colours including white, pink, yellow and orange.

Phlox 'Twinkle Star Mixed' needs a sunny spot for its flowers to give of their best. It is seen here with tagetes, royal blue lobelia and white arabis.

A good example of a one-colour border including petunias and lobelia, all in shades of mauve.

Rudbeckia (cone flower) A welcome late-flowering plant with lots of brilliant blooms in large daisy-like style. Available in shades of orange, yellow and deep red. Well-drained land, sunny or semi-sunny spot required.

Salpiglossis (painted tongue) If you can grow tender plants, here is an exotic addition with velvety, funnel-shaped flowers that are veined in strange mixtures of gold on purple, red on yellow, and yellow on red. Requires support, and pinching out. Well-drained, sheltered and sunny spot needed.

Tagetes (African marigold, French marigold) Not as popular as it once was, but still one of the most used bedding flowers where shades of yellow and orange are needed. Grows well anywhere. Deadhead to keep the display going through the summer.

Verbena Low growing, primrose-like, fragrant flowers usually available in shades of mauve, lilac and pink. Needs a good soil and a sunny spot. Pinch out young plants and deadhead regularly.

Zinnia Needs a fertile soil to produce its showy many coloured (white and shades of pink, mauve, yellow and red), daisy-like flowers. Also does best in a sunny position. A good cutting flower.

HARDY ANNUALS

These seeds are sown directly into the ground for the best results. The time to plant is when the soil is warm and dry, which will probably be in April. The warmth is needed for germination, and the soil needs to be on the dry side so that a good seed bed can be made.

The most important gardening tip is do not rush; the plants will always catch up if you have to delay planting by a few weeks because of adverse weather conditions. I once knew an old gardener who always insisted that June was the vital month – slowing down those plants that had developed too early, and speeding up the late arrivals. He also insisted that when you saw the first annual weeds developing you should plant annual flower seeds.

However, not all annuals need to be planted in the spring. Many will be much happier if planted in September and they will, of course, be earlier flowering than the April seeds. To achieve success with annuals follow these basic rules:

- The bed should be in a good sunny position and be well drained.
- The soil must be thoroughly prepared so that it comes up after raking with as fine a tilth as you can possibly achieve.
- Drills should be watered gently *before* sowing, not after the seed has been planted otherwise they might be washed so deep into the soil that they won't develop.
- The easiest but least effective planting method is just to scatter the seeds over the ground. However, it will be hard to distinguish the early growth from the weeds, and create problems when weeding and thinning. It is therefore better to prepare drills, in which the tinier seeds will need far less covering than the larger ones.
- Sow the seeds thinly – the small ones can be mixed with fine sand to ensure equal distribution.
- To ensure equal germination all seeds need to be in close contact with the soil, so the drills should be firmed down with the back of the rake or a spade.
- Drills should not mean straight lines. Each kind of seed could have its own shape – horizontal, curved or diagonal.
- Seeds will need protection from birds, so cover the surface with twigs or stretch black thread across the beds.
- Mark each area with the name of the seed planted. Don't impale the packet on a piece of wood at the end of a row. It will quickly get blown away. Instead, either

---

SOWING HARDY ANNUALS

1. Rake the soil finely.

2. Mark out the areas for each different type of seed.

3. Sow seeds very thinly in drills.

4. Cover them carefully and firm in with the back of a rake.

make a proper label or place the packet in a plastic bag before fixing it securely to a small stake.

● Thin out the seeds on a gradual basis – but do begin early and keep them to about 5 cm (2 in) apart. About 10–14 days later carry out the final thinning to the distance recommended on the seed label.

● Since most of these plants set their own seeds it is possible to raise these seedlings. Collect seedheads and thoroughly dry, before labelling and storing them in an airtight tin for use next spring. Although these seeds won't necessarily provide you with exactly the same plant as the parent, it is still an excellent and enjoyable way of raising plants.

Some interesting annuals to try out in your garden are:

Althaea (hollyhock) Best grown as an annual. Likes a sunny, sheltered spot. May need staking. Single and double flowered forms come in all colours except blue. Can fall victim to rust.

Alyssum Dwarf cushions, usually of tiny white flowers but there are other colours available. Will grow anywhere in the garden. If you have the patience to trim off dead blooms it will go on flowering for a long time. Will also re-seed itself if the old flowers are left.

Centaurea (cornflower) Once dismissed as a weed, now appreciated as a valuable annual for flowering and cutting. There are pink, red-purple, and blue and white cultivars. The soil should be well drained. May need staking and should be deadheaded regularly.

Clarkia Easy to grow, upright, needs a lightish soil, slightly acid. Does not like to be disturbed. The flowers, available in white, pinks and mauves are good for cutting, but remove bottom leaves before putting them in the water.

Dimorphotheca (Cape marigold or star of the Veldt) This is in fact perennial although it is nearly always treated as an annual. Responds best in full sun, producing lovely daisy-like, usually orange flowers all summer. Don't disturb, but do cut and remove dead heads.

Eschscholzia (Californian poppy) Full sun is essential, and a well-drained spot. The brilliant orange individual flowers do not last, but the plant flowers from June to September. It will also self-seed.

Godetia Bright, free-flowering favourites in mauves, pinks and white are colourful in the garden and good for

Clarkia is a reliable hardy annual in the border and lasts well as a cut flower.

21

Godetia will give a lasting display in a summer border.

cutting. Does best on light land in a sunny spot, and needs watering in dry conditions.

Helichrysum (straw flower) A very popular 'everlasting' flower in pink, yellow, red and rust. Full sun required. Cuttings should be taken just before the flowers fully open.

Iberis (candytuft) If you want a flower that can grow in any conditions, this is it. Excellent as edging for footpaths, or in the front of a border. Perfumed flowers in red, pink or white.

Limnanthes (poached-egg flower)
Makes a colourful, two-toned front for the border. Fern-like foliage and a flower which lives up to its common name, being white edged with a yellow centre. Likes the sun, and it will re-seed forever!

Malcolmia (Virginia stock) It will grow quickly anywhere, and blooms for weeks. The mauve, pink or white flowers smell delicious, especially in the evening.

Nemophila (baby blue eyes)
Low growing, feathery, and attractive blue flower (other colours available) for the front of a border. Don't disturb and keep watering in dry weather.

Nigella (love-in-a-mist) Once it was just misty blue but now it is multicoloured. The cornflower blue is the loveliest ('Miss Jekyll' is a popular choice). Seed pods dry well. Needs good soil.

Salvia There isn't a park in the country that doesn't have some brilliant red spikes of salvia (often called the scarlet sage) among its bedding plants. Other colours available besides red. Not too fussy about soil conditions.

Tropaeolum (nasturtium) This climbing, clambering, trailing plant goes on and on, demanding little from the garden. It has orange, yellow and red flowers. It does not need feeding and loves a poor sandy soil. Dwarf varieties growing to about 30 cm (1 ft) are available.

Viola (pansy) The dividing line between a viola and garden pansy is very narrow. The viola is harder to grow and the flowers are smaller. Useful for bedding, edging, window boxes, and hanging baskets. Water well. Deadhead regularly. Protect from slugs.

Left: Pansies add a special charm to any garden.

Opposite: *Limnanthes douglasii* is aptly called the poached-egg flower.

Below: Candytuft (*Iberis*) in shades of pink.

BIENNIALS AND PERENNIALS

Biennials are plants which you will sow this year for flowering in 12 months time. Many of the plants will re-seed and go on repeating themselves for years. They should be planted outdoors in a special nursery bed from May to July. The procedure for preparing the bed and the seed drills is just the same as for the annuals. However these plants differ in that they are planted out in the autumn in their final growing positions.

Lift the seedlings carefully and plant them in their flowering position, which should have been thoroughly prepared, and well watered. Make sure they never dry out. Among the best of the biennials are Canterbury bells (*Campanula*), forget-me-not, hollyhock, honesty, pansy, sweet William and wallflower, which will give a profusion of colour from spring through to autumn. Many of these can also be planted as annuals.

Perennials are treated in the same way, except that when the seeds germinate and the plants have been thinned and grown on, they are then planted individually into pots in the autumn. The main problem is that many perennials take years to reach a good flowering size, so unless you have extra patience and dedication ignore these plants or instead of raising from seed, buy plants already part grown. The dedicated gardener who ignores this warning will benefit from such marvellous plants as the primulas and polyanthus, lupin, delphinium, and geum, all of which grow well from seed.

Biennial plants which haven't been mentioned in the list of annuals, and which are well worth considering include:

Bellis (daisy)   There are many varieties of *Bellis perennis* in white, pink and red,

Low-growing *Campanula portenschlagiana* is suitable for the front of a border or rock garden.

that make ideal edging plants or for growing in rockeries. Easily grown.

Campanula (Canterbury bells) These are produced in many shades of blue, pink and white. Protect from slugs, stake, and deadhead when the flowers fade.

Cheiranthus (wallflowers) The fragrant flower, synonymous with spring, comes in red, pink, yellow, purple, white and cream. Sunny spot required; and pinch out the young plants before planting.

Digitalis (foxglove) Tall spikes in a great range of colours as well as the traditional purple. Needs lots of water and is happy in a moist, shaded spot.

Lunaria (honesty) Although you will see most of these in shades of purple, white and pink are also available. The seed pods dry well for winter arrangements.

Myosotis (forget-me-not) You can buy it in other colours, but the blue is still the most popular with most of us. Will grow

well in light shade, but do not let it dry out.

Perennials, as pointed out earlier, are generally better purchased as plants and then propagated as cuttings or root divisions. However, there are some that are successfully and easily raised from seed. Many are mentioned in the chapter, *Flowers for Cutting*. The primula and the geum are special cases.

Primula (primrose, polyanthus) No garden would be complete without them. The dividing line between the huge variety of flowers in this group is not really clear. Some need bog-like conditions, others are almost alpine in their size and treatment, and the old garden strains ask few favours and provide a wide range of sizes and colours. But don't despair – from a packet of seeds you can get a wonderful selection. In particular try the Pacific or the Goldlace strains. Since primulas are not long-lasting plants, it is better to grow replacements from seed every year. However, if you have a particularly delightful plant propagate by careful division. In the garden the plants thrive in partial shade.

Geum (avens) If you want a dense, weed-smothering plant for the summer this has few rivals. The flowers are bright, and come in shades of red, orange and yellow. A rich soil is vital to its success, and staking will later be necessary. Clumps should be cut back to the ground once flowering has finished, and like the primula the plant is not long lasting. Clumps can be divided every few years.

CUTTINGS

Taking a cutting from a favourite plant and watching it grow, is one of the gardener's greatest joys. To the true enthusiast a cutting is just about anything – a tiny snip from the tip of a fuchsia or a geranium; a shoot from the base of a delphinium or peony; or a heel cutting taken from any medium hard-wood plant. All can be encouraged to grow, you will have more successes than failures.

There are four kinds of cutting. The *tip* cuttings are very short pieces of wood that have not yet flowered, and which are soft at the top and quite firm at the base.

Primulas come in a wide range of colours. The old-fashioned Goldlace types seen here are becoming increasingly popular.

Basal cuttings are taken from the base of the plant – they are usually young shoots which can be pulled or cut away.

Heel cuttings are obtained by removing a side shoot from the main stem in such a way that a piece of wood remains at the bottom, which is called a 'heel'.

Hardwood cuttings of shrubs are taken in autumn and planted outdoors. Choose well ripened shoots and trim to about 25 cm (10 in). Provided you take the appropriate cutting from the relevant plant and treat it correctly, you will have few problems. The planting stage should be handled as follows.

Having taken the cutting, remove the bottom sets of leaves which would otherwise be in danger of being buried under the soil. You must leave sufficient leaves above the soil for the plant to breathe.

Next, dip the base of the cutting into a rooting hormone compound, shaking off the excess if powder is used. You should then make a suitable hole with a dibber or a pencil in a firmed, sterile potting medium, and gently ease in the cutting. If there is an interval between the cutting being taken and planted it should be kept in water, but you ought to avoid this.

The cutting must be kept in a humid atmosphere which can be created by covering it with a plastic bag (half a plastic soft drink bottle makes a good cover for smaller pots). Don't be tempted to look too soon for a root since cuttings don't like being tampered with. Leave the cutting for some weeks and if the new growth has appeared then a gentle tug will let you know whether it has rooted. Any leaves that turn yellow, fall off or start to rot should be quickly removed.

The cutting will grow on quite happily for some weeks, and when it has rooted sufficiently it should be potted on into a suitably sized container – probably a 7.5 cm (3 in) pot – filled with potting compost. If you have a number of cuttings consider raising them in a rooting bag or cold frame. If you intend taking a lot of cuttings then it will be worthwhile buying a propagator.

TAKING TIP CUTTINGS

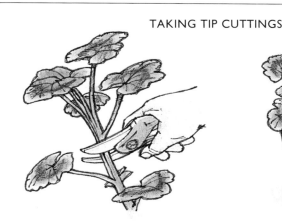

1. These can be taken from any non-flowering side shoot. Trim away lower leaves that would otherwise be under the soil.

2. Dip cutting in hormone rooting powder and insert in a pot immediately. You can plant on four or five cuttings in a small pot.

25

BASAL CUTTINGS

1. Young cuttings at the base of the plant can be pulled away carefully or trimmed with a knife.

2. Trim across the base and remove leaves from lower half of cuttings.

3. Insert in a hole close to the edge of the pot and water in very gently.

Probably the most successful cuttings can be taken for the flower garden from many of the plants mentioned later in the book (see Chaper 5), but the most popular, fuchsia and pelargonium, deserve special attention here.

Fuchsia

Fuchsias are such attractive plants and come in such a wide variety of colours and shapes that they are the subject of many specialist books. They have a large following of enthusiasts and are universally popular for planting in hanging baskets and containers, either on their own or in combination with other plants, to give a display which continues throughout the summer.

The major drawback, however, is that some fuchsias are so tender that they must be sheltered even in the summer. And most hybrid plants will need protection in the winter or be taken under cover. However, in warmer parts of the country and in mild winters some of the special outdoor varieties survive quite well.

There are hundreds of different fuchsias which can be grown as trailing plants, or trained to form bushes, pyramids or standards, and their classification is complex. One nursery which specializes in fuchsias actually lists 487 cultivars, and the number is still growing! However, it is enough to be aware of the delightful white, red, mauve, violet, pink, cream, rose, and bicolors that are available, mixing grace with a distinctiveness unrivalled by any other flower.

Propagation Propagating the fuchsia is almost child's play, and involves taking either soft tip cuttings about 8 cm (3 in) long in early summer or harder wood later in the year. In the case of the tips use nonflowered wood which can be planted outdoors in pots or at the foot of the mother plant. A cold frame or a propagator is, of course, better, but if you do not have one it is easy to improvise. The plants will usually root within three weeks. With hardwood cuttings, which can be taken after pruning, trim them to about 12 cm (5 in) dip them in rooting hormone and place them in a propagator. They need to be kept at a temperature of about 7°C (45°F).

If you want to begin collecting fuchsia you should not find any trouble purchasing several different varieties, recently well rooted, at a reasonable price. Some of the interesting varieties that the beginner could try include miniatures such as 'Lady Thumb' (sepals reddish carmine, with corolla white veined with carmine), and 'Papoose' (sepals bright red, with corolla very dark purple); or prizewinners such as

HEEL CUTTINGS

Break off cutting with a heel of older wood, trim neatly and plant.

HARDWOOD CUTTINGS

Trim cuttings to 25 cm (10 in) and insert in V shaped trench in sheltered border.

'Mieke Meursing' (red sepals, corolla pale pink), and 'Display' (sepals rose pink, corolla deep pink); or the very new and exciting 'Pink La Campanella' (a mixture of pale and dark carmine sepals, with white markings and a bright magenta corolla); or a hardy variety such as 'Garden News' (pink sepals, majenta corolla).

All you need to remember is that there are different types – outdoor, bedding and greenhouse. The outdoors are generally hardy in most of Great Britain. They should be left to die down of their own volition rather than being cut down in the autumn. Bedding varieties need to be taken indoors in the winter and transferred to pots. Store in a shed with plenty of light, do not feed and water very sparingly. They can be planted out again in the spring. The greenhouse varieties are best treated as indoor plants, but in a really good summer they can be placed outdoors on a warm patio.

Pelargoniums

Nearly everyone uses the term geranium to cover this wide range of plants, although the enthusiast would be much happier if its proper name was used. For the present, I will call them all geraniums. Botanically there is a slight distinction between the pelargonium and the geranium – the former has five stamens, irregular petals and a tube for nectar; the geranium does not have the tube, and has six or more stamens with a more regular shaped leaf. But some of these distinctions are now being blurred by the arrival of many new cultivars.

Cultivar is the word denoting a cultivated variety, but the various hybrids and cultivars are still widely referred to as varieties.

Whatever name you call it by, the geranium is a wonderful flower. For many it is *the* flower of the windowsill (often being planted in a lovely old Victorian style pot), the essential blaze of colour in large bedding schemes, the long-lasting trailing flower in hanging baskets and tubs, and the provider of subtle foliage in the border. For all of these situations there is a different type – bedding geraniums, fancyleaf geraniums, regal perlargoniums and ivy-leaf perlargoniums, each with its own characteristic that will become obvious to the gardener as the plants begin to grow and flower.

The only problem with these plants is that they need a frost-free environment, which means that at the end of the summer and before the first frosts they must be moved indoors. From now on they should be given just a minute amount of watering until late spring, when the threat of frost has passed. A bright spot in a shed or under the staging in a greenhouse with good wrapping is usually good enough.

For growing geraniums you need a sandy, rich loam, good sunshine, and miserly watering. To keep it in top condition don't allow the aphids and whitefly to settle on it, and give the roots an occasional feeding with a soluble or liquid fertilizer to give the plant a boost.

This is another plant which is easily raised from cuttings – either stem cuttings (any time after flowering) or non-flowered tips, usually in the early summer. By using one of these methods you can have new plants developing from May to September.

Propagation Take a cutting about 7.5 cm (3 in) long in spring or early summer. I have always found that non-flowering tip cuttings are best because the growth is active and therefore encourages rooting. However, flowered cuttings will provide you with a good plant, though in a slower time. In either case trim stem to just below a leaf base and remove the lower leaves. These cuttings are among the easiest plants in the world to root, and even the top rose growers constantly express the hope that one day they will produce roses that can root as easily as a geranium.

These red geraniums (or pelargoniums) have attractively 'zoned' foliage, and are seen here with white alyssum.

BULBS, CORMS, TUBERS AND RHIZOMES

The majority of bulbs and corms spread to form clumps, which will eventually require lifting and dividing every few years. The best time to do this is after flowering, when the foliage has died down. Lift the clumps carefully and divide the bulbs. Replant the biggest to provide next year's flowers. The small bulblets or cormlets, which are attached to the main bulbs, should be detached; these can be planted elsewhere in the garden where they can be allowed to grow in their own time. It may take two to three years for them to reach the flowering stage, and when they in turn are lifted the same process can again be adopted.

Rhizomes are underground stems which produce shoots and roots, and they can be increased, usually in the summer, by dividing and cutting. Trim away any rotten or diseased parts and then divide the rhizome into sections, each one containing roots and foliage or buds. Then plant the sections at the same depth as the original plant. Bearded irises can be increased this way. The easiest plant in this group to divide and propagate is the lily of the valley.

Probably the best known tuberous plants are the dahlias (see page 66) and the tuberous begonias (as opposed to the half-hardy annual, the bedding begonia).

Begonias

These give a wonderful display of colour all summer long – provided that you can be sure they have a super rich soil, plenty of sunshine, and constant root watering when they are flowering. They make magnificent bedding plants with large rose-like blooms in just about every summer colour. *B. pendula* with its long, drooping stems is ideal for window boxes and hanging baskets.

The tubers can be divided when the young growth is beginning. Take pieces from the sides of the main tuber very carefully, and plant them separately in potting compost. Keep them under cover until all risk of frost has passed. Then they can be planted out where they will need a liquid fertilizer. Remove stems when foliage has died down, lift tubers and store away from frost over winter.

PRESERVING FLOWERS

As well as the flowers that bear the name 'everlasting' – acroclinium, helichrysum and limonium or statice – there are many others that can be used for drying for winter decoration and in dried flower arrangements. They include larkspur, love-lies-bleeding, achillea, delphiniums, molucella, astilbes, sedums, ballota, even rosebuds.

The flowers should be picked just as the blooms are opening and before they reach maturity. Tie them in small bunches and hang them upside down in a dry dark cupboard, shed or attic where there is a good circulation of air; darkness prevents the colours from fading. Leave them alone if you can until they are needed for decoration. Grasses are particularly useful when dried in this way, and they provide graceful backgrounds for arrangements of other dried material.

Many people use the pressing method to preserve ferns, ivy, bracken, large leaves of trees or shrubs. The leaves should be laid flat between sheets of newspaper, making sure they are not overlapping. Weigh them down with equal pressure all over, and leave until completely dry. Leaves of trees, and shrubs and herbaceous plants can be placed between sheets of newspaper and then ironed. Treat hosta leaves in this manner. You will find that because drying with an iron is quicker, the leaf colour will be well preserved. The leaves can then be mounted on florists' wire and used in arrangements.

Tuberous begonias are truly magnificent summer bedders. Here they are interplanted with silver-foliaged Senecio and spider plants (*Chlorophytum*).

PROPAGATING BULBS, CORMS AND RHIZOMES

In the summer after flowering, gently lift rhizomes. Divide into sections with a sharp knife so that each section has some roots below and growth above. Replant at the same depth as original plant.

The small cormlets around the base of a gladiolus corm can be detached and, if grown on, will flower within two years.

Bulbs are easily propagated. Lift the bulb cluster after the foliage has died down and break off the side bulbs. Tinier bulblets can be planted in an out-of-the-way spot where they can grow on for two or three years.

PLANTS IN CONTAINERS

This type of gardening is ideal if you have only a small amount of space as just about any plant, from a tiny alpine to a large standard rose, can be grown in a container and often plants will take on a different persona when displayed in this way. Perhaps they become more noticeable because they are rather more isolated from their immediate surroundings than when they are planted in a bed or border. In this way the true beauty of each flower can be appreciated in all its detail.

For instance, a large day lily (*Hemerocallis*) growing tall among the trailing foliage of a ground covering plant will prove a real eye-catcher. You can easily pick your own colour schemes and make your container plants match or tone in with the surrounding plants. Fuchsias come in a wonderful range of pinks, reds and mauves and are particularly suited to planting in tubs, pots and window boxes. The floribunda roses are also ideal for displaying in containers and 'Trumpeter' (red) and 'Korresia' (yellow) are specially recommended.

Hydrangeas in blue or pink, mophead or lacecap, will bloom for a long period while all the summer-flowering bedding plants are suitable. Particular favourites include ageratums, begonias, geraniums (pelargoniums), nasturtiums, pansies, petunias and Sweet Williams. Bulbs of all types can be used to give a good display and are invaluable for filling tubs with colour in the spring.

SELECTING A CONTAINER

There are many types of containers available in all manner of styles and materials including wood, plastic, stone and terracotta. The plastic and glassfibre containers, although frequently despised for not being traditional, are often good value and preferable where ease of movement is required as they are very light. This makes them ideal for use in roof gardens or other places where heavier containers could cause problems. They are also available in many different shapes, including reproductions of the period vases and urns that decorate the great gardens. Always remember that when they are planted up they will look quite different with foliage softening their contours. The classical stone and terra-cotta containers are always beautiful but more expensive. Concrete containers can be used as substitutes with success as these now come in a range of attractive designs. Wooden containers provide a good natural and often neutral accompaniment to plants on a patio. Remember it is your choice, so select those you like and that suit your purse – but do check the range first before coming to a decision.

PLANTING A CONTAINER

When planting up a container, be it tub, windowbox or pot, it is essential to ensure adequate drainage, so in addition to the drainage holes it is advisable to put a layer of broken crocks or pebbles in the bottom. Then fill the container with compost to suit the needs of the particular plants – lime-free or ericaceous compost for heathers, rhododendrons or camellias, for example. John Innes potting compost No 3 or an equivalent is best for roses or shrubs that are going to remain in the same pot for years, whereas John Innes potting compost No 2 or an equivalent will be adequate for bedding plants that are changed annually. A soilless compost will dry out quicker but is lighter, so more suited for hanging baskets, window boxes or in containers that will be moved about (taken indoors or into the greenhouse for winter). Once the plant is in position it is important to keep it adequately watered as the compost will dry out faster than the soil in a bed or border. A soluble fertilizer should also be applied according to the manufacturers' instructions to give the plants a boost in the growing season.

Each spring the top couple of centimetres (1 in) of compost in a container should be removed and replaced by fresh potting compost. Remember, too, that many shrubs and roses will outgrow their container and need moving on into something larger after a few years.

POSITIONING THE CONTAINER

It is very important to find the best place for your containers. Try to place them where they will get at least some sunshine most days, but not where the plants will be scorched by the direct summer sun all day long. Remember that in a hot summer any container will dry out quickly and therefore will need a great deal of watering, so check the compost every day. Make sure that your containers harmonize with the rest of the garden whether they stand alone as a focal point or are grouped together, and that, if you need to move them frequently, they are easy to handle.

HANGING BASKETS

Bright summer flowers, that will generally be viewed from below, can provide lovely spot colour against a stone, brick or concrete wall. Don't plant sparingly. When you think you have enough in the basket put in one more! As a general rule of thumb, plant trailing subjects around the edge and more upright plants in the centre. Make sure you hang the baskets where you can reach them for watering as they dry out very quickly indeed and may need watering more than once a day in hot summer weather.

Among the plants that do well in hanging baskets are trailing geraniums (pelargoniums) and pendulous fuchsias, both of which will tumble their flowers over the side of the basket and provide longlasting colour. Other plants that give great value include lobelias, creeping Jenny (*Lysimachia nummularia*), petunias, and trailing nasturtiums.

Fuchsias, petunias and trailing lobelia provide a show of summer colour in this window box.

WINDOW BOXES

The deciding factor in planting up a window box is the amount of sun it will get. For best effect place it on a south-facing sill but for a less than sunny spot or even for a north-facing wall look for plants like Busy Lizzies, Californian poppies (*Eschscholzia*) and nasturtiums that will thrive in shade.

Window boxes can be produced with a lovely seasonal effect by using low grow-ing tulips or daffodils in the spring and then changing to summer-flowering plants.

There are many lovely plants to choose from for summer effect in a sunny spot. Geraniums are, of course, one of the favourites but try tightly planted minia-ture roses ('Rise 'n' Shine' is a yellow variety that does very well) on their own. Other flowering plants that will brighten any window box include ageratums, bego-nias, trailing campanulas, fuchsias, helio-trope and petunias.

In autumn heathers (winter-flowering *Erica herbacea* cultivars) and winter cherry (*Solanum capsicastrum*) provide colour and an interplanting of variegated ivy or ivy-leaf pelargoniums will trail attractively and add interest throughout the year.

PLANTING A HANGING BASKET

1. Line the basket with a generous layer of sphagnum moss or perforated black polythene before filling with a lightweight potting compost.

2. Plant trailing plants, such as lobelia, through the sides of the basket so they will cover the basket and hang down attractively.

3. Finally plant the top of the basket with some more upright subjects to give height. Plant closely and generously, and soak well before hanging up.

CREATING A BORDER

The wonderful thing about gardening is that you are free to create as you wish. Lovers of shrubs can establish a shrub border; wonderful spot beds can be made from annuals; and roses can be spectacular when grouped together. But surely the most interesting sight of all must be the border that provides a little bit of everything – annuals, perennials, shrubs, bulbs, and roses. Most call it the mixed border, although 'versatile' might be a far better word because it suggests both colourful flowers and attractive foliage right through the year. Certainly the mixed border must rank as the most rewarding feature of the small to average sized garden. The possibilities are enormous. Just consider growing campanulas side by side with an elegant group of regal lilies,

or having dramatic large-flowered delphiniums towering over old fashioned pinks, all close beside the soft coloured bearded iris.

A border of mixed or herbaceous plants will provide flowers and foliage for cutting, and plants that can be left in position for a number of years. Apart from pruning and dividing, they demand little work. However, it has to be said that these benefits will only be reaped by those who put the initial work into the planning, designing and preparing. That might sound horrifying to the new gardener, but remember it can be a pleasure.

Such a border can be planted anywhere, even in open lawn, although where it can be viewed from each side there will be more restrictions on the types of plants to

be used. Most usually a background wall, fence or hedge will provide the necessary frame, and will also provide a windbreak which is important when taller plants are being grown.

POINTS TO REMEMBER

The first point to remember about any wall, hedge or fence is that room should be left between the back of your border and the 'frame' should you need to walk along there when making repairs. You may need to paint a wall or fence, or clip a hedge. Also remember that hedges have hungry roots which can deprive the border plants of vital nutrients. The ideal gap between the two should be 45 cm (18 in), and if you can lay slabs, stones or any type of path

An herbaceous border should be a source of flowers and foliage for cutting through much of the year. This border is given height by rambler roses ('American Pillar') trained up rustic tripods.

Lilac provides fragrant flowers in late spring and early summer. This is the single 'Souvenir de Louis Spaeth'.

then access will be that much easier.

Another important point to remember about any border, whether it be shrub, mixed or herbaceous, is that it needs sun, so a south facing position is best. If this is impossible do not worry, for good borders can be created just about anywhere. The basic requirement is that the border is placed in the sunniest part of the garden. It also needs a certain amount of space to be effective. The minimum requirements are 1.2 × 3.7 m (4 × 12 ft). If the border is any smaller than this you should restrict the number of plants used to six or seven different types, ensuring they provide a good mix of flowers and foliage over a long period.

If you have more space it is possible to create one of a wide range of borders, incorporating varying widths and curves, which will be far more interesting than a border of straight lines. As I have already mentioned, one of the great advantages of a mixed or herbaceous border is that you can change it from year to year. And, as you become more adventurous and knowledgeable, it will be possible to create bolder and ever more spectacular displays.

There are, of course, many variations of borders apart from the herbaceous and mixed. The dedicated planner can devise a highly scented garden or a border devoted to one type of plant (such as the rose), or one-colour – delphiniums, dahlias, chrysanthemums and roses, among those that immediately come to mind, but there are so many others that the gardener can be spoilt for choice.

A scented garden has its own obvious pleasures, and despite the cries that scent is being lost by modern flower breeders there are many, many different types of flowers that can be used effectively in this way. The heady scent of wallflowers, the lovely mignonette and, of course night-scented-stock, are all excellent choices. But there are many more which can be appreciated from spring to winter, and they include the white *Nicotiana* (tobacco plant) and many forms of lilac, lavender, lily of the valley, the old fashioned border carnations, honeysuckle, viburnum, sweet peas, and jasmine.

Nicotiana 'Lime Green', like other tobacco plants, is at its most fragrant in the evening.

33

FLOWER GARDENING

Some of the rules for creating a mixed border are:

● Careful soil preparation is vital. There is nothing to beat a well dug and fertilized bed.

● Soggy land or a sunless position are the two great handicaps. Try for good drainage and full sun.

● When selecting plants make sure that you have allowed space for those that are rampant growers and which, after a time, may well suffocate slower growing plants placed near them.

● Place taller growing plants (such as weigela or fuchsia) at the back of the border, with the lower ones in front. The middle area is reserved for the iris, lupin, stocks and other colourful average size flowers.

● Try to keep the ground between plants open by hoeing and weeding.

● A mulch of organic material – peat or well-rotted compost for instance – will keep down weeds and also conserve water. On the edges of beds a mulch of small forest bark can be very effective and looks quite good too. Certainly it can save a lot of hoeing.

● When cutting flowers for house decoration go very easy on new plants. The loss of stems and greenery can harm next year's growth. This will be obvious on perennials and even newly planted roses. If you want a flower from a first-year plant, then cut it with as little stem as possible and do not remove any leaves.

● Remove flower heads once they have faded, which will give the plants a chance of repeat flowering later in the season. Do not break them off – use a sharp scissors or better still shears or secateurs.

● Do not remove any foliage until it has died down.

● If you wish to move a plant in the border wait until autumn, but in the meantime identify it and make a note on the label of where you intend to place it.

● Wear gloves. There may be times when they will be awkward but for safety's sake it is much better to wear them constantly.

THE ANNUAL BORDER

Annuals are superb for bringing colour into a developing area, such as a shrub or herbaceous border. In order to make them

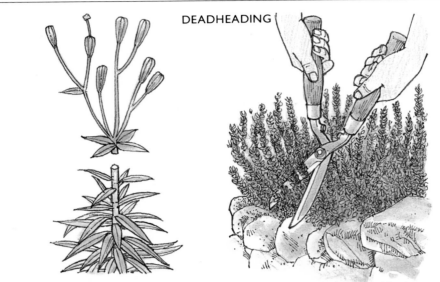

DEADHEADING

Removing the spent flowers from most plants will encourage another flush of bloom. Cut just below the flowerhead.

Heathers should be trimmed back as soon as their flowers have faded. Prune back any straggly shoots but do not cut into old wood.

Left: A traditional display of annuals brings brilliant colour to the garden in summer.

Opposite: One of the best-known borders with a colour theme – the red border at Hidcote, Gloucestershire.

truly effective they need to be spread boldly and in drifts, so that their colour isn't diluted in dribs and drabs. The rigid planning of tall flowers at the back and low ones in the front need not be adhered to in this instance – annuals of different heights, planted perhaps by colour and not by scale look far more interesting, natural and informal.

What has to be remembered is that making a border exclusively from annuals can be something of a chore and will not, of course, last beyond one season. But in a new and developing garden the annual is vital in providing almost instant colour. A box of hardened-off annuals can be transferred into the garden to give good colour and cover for quite a long period through the summer and autumn. If the faded flower heads are snipped off many plants will rebloom.

BEDDING OPTIONS

With these flowers or shrubs the gardener is not restricted to a long line that most people call a border, whether it be one for herbaceous or mixed plants. The same sort of flowers can be used in an island bed, except that here the taller plants will be used in the middle and they must be selected with some care so that they do not throw other plants into their shade. A smaller bed may be prepared for annuals, and these too will be viewed from all sides.

Raised beds can be very effective where a line has to be broken or where the gardener finds that bending or stooping is difficult. The raised bed can be created using a retaining wall, the area being filled in with a well mixed soil suitable for whatever plants are to be grown. For instance, peat beds are very useful for growing lime-hating plants, and if they consist of peat blocks they will also provide slots into which small heathers or ferns can be placed effectively.

Rock gardens are a very specialized part of a garden and their success depends on the amount of work that is put into them (see pages 81 to 88).

USING BULBS

There is a wide range of bulbous plants that fits into all these planting situations, from the stately hybridized gladioli to the daintier and highly fragrant autumn flowering *Acidanthera* (in fact, now classified as *Gladiolus callianthus*). Make sure that you know the eventual height that the flower will reach before planting it – some quite small bulbs can still produce tall plants.

It is a mistake to believe that all bulbs are trouble free, for they need good soil preparation and some care through the years. For instance, gladioli bulbs need lifting before winter sets in, while the others do need careful planting, good soil and feeding, just like other plants.

There are some bulbous plants that fit into a border more easily than others. The gladioli, for instance, does not always mix happily with border flowers although the interesting range of butterfly gladioli are much happier in this situation. And for a real eye-catcher there is the crown imperial, *Fritillaria imperialis*, not unlike its dainty cousins in the same genus. With its yellow or deep orange bell-like flowers circling the top of each 90 cm (3 ft) tall and quite thick stem, it is a plant that needs careful placing, but you can be sure it will create interest especially if you plant a small group of about six or seven together.

Freesias are always a delight because of their fragrance, and the outdoor variety presents a lovely display in the late summer and autumn. They require a dry, warm spot, and like most of these bulbous plants need to be kept watered. But the same message must be repeated – avoid constantly waterlogged soil. The well-drained, fertile piece of ground is where bulbous plants will grow best.

SHRUBS IN THE BORDER

Some of the most remarkable gardens are devoted exclusively to one or two colours – the red border at Hidcote, the white garden at Sissinghurst are just two very famous examples.

Beverly Nichols once had part of his garden planted with grey or bluish silver roses and another part devoted to white flowers.

Here are just a few ideas that you may

One of the most stately of bulbous flowering plants is the crown imperial, *Fritillaria imperialis* 'Lutea'.

care to adopt. Divided up into red, yellow, pink and violet, blue and mauve, and white flowered shrubs, you should be able to pick out easily the plants for your own favourite colour scheme.

The emphasis has been placed on flowering shrubs because they will provide a permanent framework in the garden and a setting for bulbs, herbaceous perennials and annuals with their more flamboyant flowers. Flowering shrubs can be also used alone for a more subtle effect. Many of these will provide additional year-round interest with fruits following flowers, silver or evergreen foliage and fiery autumn colour.

Of course there are a number of plants which come in a wide range of colours, particularly the roses (covered in detail in their own chapter – pages 51 to 63) and the rhododendron hybrids. No garden would be complete without a few shrubs, so here are some favourites that have proven

themselves over the years and which will make ideal additions to the mixed border in any garden.

RED FLOWERED SHRUBS

Azaleas These are now included in the genus *Rhododendron* but are still widely sold under their old name. These are, on the whole, much daintier plants and more suited to growing in small gardens. The evergreen or Japanese azaleas are low growing and quite adaptable, producing masses of flowers in May.

Look out for 'Addy Werry', 'Mother's Day' or the orange-red 'Orange Beauty'. The deciduous types are taller growing and include the triumphant 'Koster's Brilliant Red' among them. They need a lime-free soil, a sheltered site, light shade and plenty of moisture as they are shallow rooting. Propagate from seed or from layering low-growing stems.

Chaenomeles Better known as japonica, this early spring flowering shrub is perfect for training against a fence or wall. The best red-flowering variety is 'Knap Hill Scarlet' which flowers from March to May with golden fruits in autumn, but there are many to choose from of this hue. It does well in partial shade but is at its best in full sun. Trim back in summer after flowering. Propagate from suckers or from heeled cuttings taken in summer.

Enkianthus The pagoda bush is renowned for its brilliant red and yellow flowers late in spring and also for its glorious autumn colour. *E. campanulatus* grows to about 2.4 m (8 ft) high. It needs a lime-free soil and light shade. The only pruning necessary is to cut away any old or damaged wood. Propagate from heeled cuttings in summer.

Escallonia (see page 41) 'Crimson Spire' is a good red form.

Potentilla (see page 40) 'Gibson's Scarlet' is an excellent red-flowered cultivar.

Rhododendron Like the azaleas they come in nearly every colour imaginable. There are many to choose from in various shades of red. The hardy hybrids are evergreen and need little in the way of pruning. Among the best red hybrids are 'Britannia', 'Cynthia' – vigorous and dark red, scarlet 'Doncaster', 'John Walter' and crimson 'Lord Roberts'. Among the dwarf growers to look out for is the dark red 'Elizabeth' which reaches between 90 and 120 cm (3–4 ft) and carries large trumpet-like flowers in April. They need a good acid soil and benefit from a spring mulch to conserve soil moisture in summer. Plant in a sheltered position, preferably in light shade.

Ribes (flowering currant) Search out some of the named varieties, rather than the species, *R. sanguineum*, the red

'Pulborough Scarlet' or the deep crimson, 'King Edward VII' are among the best. These are quick to establish and grow well in most soils reaching 1.8 m (6 ft) in height. Prune back after flowering and cut out any old, unproductive wood. To propagate take hardwood cuttings, about 30 cm (1 ft) long, and plant out in open ground in autumn.

Rosa (see pages 51 to 63)

Weigela This is a useful shrub for the border that comes in a wide range of colours including red. 'Bristol Ruby' is perhaps the best of the reds, flowering as it does in spring, summer and often again in autumn. It likes a humus-rich soil and a sunny or lightly shaded position. It may reach over 1.8 m (6 ft), but is very tolerant of clipping. In fact it makes an attractive informal hedge. Propagate from heeled cuttings in summer or from hardwood cuttings taken at the end of autumn.

BUYING PLANTS

Container grown plants
There is a difference between container grown plants, and container stuffed plants. Container grown plants should be just that – the plant should have been raised from a seed or a cutting, and then potted on to reach its final destination in the garden centre or store as a developing young plant. Stuffed plants have been lifted from the ground and then placed in containers when already fully grown. Obviously the shock of such a transfer can damage the plant enormously, so always look for plants that seem happy in their containers.

The good plant will be healthy looking with bright foliage – it will be well labelled and will look as though it has been growing successfully in the container. If there are signs of moss or small weeds in it don't worry, they will be a further indication that it is a container-grown plant. Wilted or yellowing leaves, signs of pests, dried out compost or a split or broken container are all signs that this is a poor plant, and best avoided.

Pre-packed plants
Pre-packed plants are now widely available. These are bare rooted plants, packed in a plastic covering, with some moist peat or compost covering the roots. The main problem when considering them is that the packaging makes it very hard to see what you are buying, and the plant could be in a poor state from the warm conditions on the sales bench. Good stores will make sure that they only carry fresh stock. If you can see the plant, and there are signs of premature growth, shrivelled stems or small white roots, then reject it. The best plant is one that is completely dormant and looks healthy and strong.

Trays of plants
These trays are commonplace, and vary in quality enormously. Seedlings may be dried out and dying, they may be thin and spindly, have yellowing leaves, or be so far advanced that the roots are growing out through the base of the tray. What the gardener needs are sturdy, compact little plants that are

growing evenly. Many of these plants will also be seen offered in bunches and wrapped in paper. You should only buy them if you know they are absolutely fresh, and you can plant them immediately. Always select a full tray or a section of a tray, rather than loosely wrapped plants.

Seeds
The great value of buying seeds is that you can get a far greater range of annuals and biennials than if you are depending on the purchase of pre-grown bedding plants. But make sure that you will be using the seeds fairly soon. Read the instructions thoroughly and make sure that the plant is for you. Many people believe that in purchasing seeds the plants will flower in a short time. This is not true. Many of the more beautiful plants that you can grow from seeds need a whole year, in which they must be transferred from their initial growing place into containers, before being planted out in their flowering positions the following year.

YELLOW FLOWERED SHRUBS

Berberis (barberry) These shrubs carry yellow to orange flowers in late spring and summer. They also carry very sharp prickles, so beware! There are many different kinds to choose from and all are easy to grow in most garden soils. *B. darwinii* is evergreen and one of the best for flowers, followed in autumn by almost black berries. It grows to 1.8 m (6 ft) or more.

B. wilsoniae is lower growing and deciduous with translucent pink to red berries in autumn.

No regular pruning is necessary but every few years they benefit from thinning out and removing the old wood. Propagate species from seed or cuttings taken in summer.

Buddleia *B. globosa* has small ball-like heads of fragrant yellow-orange flowers in June. This shrub can grow to 4.5 m (15 ft). Lightly prune after flowering to keep in shape and prevent straggly growth forming. It thrives in most garden soils but prefers full sun. Propagate from seed or from hardwood cuttings.

Chimonanthus A deciduous shrub that is known as winter-sweet. This is a very good name because it tells you that the plant will produce very fragrant flowers, yellow with purple centres in winter. It may take some time for the plant to become established, so be patient. It will eventually reach 3 m (10 ft) and needs a sunny, well-drained spot. Best grown from seed.

Corylus (hazel) *C. avellana* 'Contorta' grows into a small tree about 3 m (10 ft) high although it may reach double that. If you want an unusual plant this is the one for you! Its branches are so contorted that it was once described as Harry Lauder's walking stick. The yellow catkins are a welcome arrival in the garden in January and February, just before the arrival of the daffodils. *C. avellana* 'Aurea' has yellow foliage and a more shrub-like habit. Hazels will grow in most places including open, windy or partially shaded sites. Propagate from suckers. Pruning is a simple task; just cut away old, exhausted branches in early spring to encourage new shoots.

Left: *Berberis darwinii*, evergreen in flower. It carries nearly black berries in autumn.

Opposite: 'Goldsworth Yellow' is a particularly hardy rhododendron hybrid.

Enkianthus (see page 37) This shrub comes with yellow flowers as well as red.

Forsythia Sometimes this is called golden bells or the leafless tree. Both these descriptions are apt at some time during its seasonal cycle. Certainly the yellow flowers on the leafless branches brighten up every spring at just the time when colour is sorely needed. Don't over-prune. Cut back stems that have produced flowers and, if heavier pruning is needed, shorten some of the stems. It usually reaches about 2.4 m (8 ft) and is easily raised from cuttings taken after flowering.

Hippophae (sea buckthorn) *H. rhamnoides* is a spiny shrub with silver foliage. It is perfect for hedging or screening in windy places, especially by the sea. It has insignificant yellow flowers and is grown for its orange berries. To ensure a good crop you must grow at least one male and one female plant although one male to three females gives a better show. The great advantage of this shrub is that the berries remain untouched right through the late autumn and winter. It grows well in most soils and tolerates sun or shade. An occasional trimming back is the only pruning necessary. It can be grown from seed in autumn.

Hypericum An attractive group of shrubs with golden yellow flowers in summer and early autumn. They range from the invasive and ground covering rose of Sharon to 'Hidcote' which can top 1.5 m (5 ft). *H. inodorum* 'Elstead' reaches about 1 m (3 ft) and forms lustrous red berries after flowering. Hypericums suit most well-drained soils and grow well in sun or light shade. Prune back in spring and propagate from heeled cuttings.

Lonicera (honeysuckle)   Fragrant flow-ered climbing plants, suitable for training over walls and fences or up tripods or pillars in the border. They grow well in most soils but prefer a sunny spot. *L. japonica* 'Halliana' is a vigorous evergreen with yellow and white flowers; *L. periclymenum* 'Belgica' and 'Serotina' are the early and late flowering Dutch honeysuckles with pink and yellow flowers. The winter honeysuckle, *L. × purpusii* bears pale yellow flowers in winter and spring. Propagate from hard-wood cuttings in autumn.

Mahonia   These shrubs grow well in most places and are easy to care for. They have good evergreen foliage and bright yellow, fragrant flowers followed by dark blue fruits. Plant in shady sites, under trees or in full sun – they look good all the year round. *M. aquifolium* (often called the Oregon grape) is small and bushy, reach-ing about 1 m (3 ft), with foliage that turns bronze in autumn. *M. japonica* is taller and

Hypericum 'Hidcote' produces large golden flowers through summer into autumn.

more upright, growing to 1.8 m (6 ft) with flowers from mid-winter into spring. 'Charity' is a very good upright shrub reaching 2.4 m (8 ft) with very large sprays of flowers. Mahonias require little in the way of pruning. Species can be raised from seed.

Phlomis Attractive grey-green foliage and abundant yellow pea-like flowers in June, *P. fruticosa* needs a sheltered spot away from danger of hard frosts. It is wide spreading and generally reaches about 90 cm (3 ft) high. It fits well into most borders, especially in association with other silver-leaved plants. It is ideal for dry places and looks good tumbling over a wall. Cut back old or damaged wood in spring. Propagate from cuttings taken in early summer and rooted under cover.

Rosa (see pages 51 to 63)

Santolina (cotton lavender) A sunny well-drained site is essential for this shrub that carries silver-grey foliage and, in summer, yellow button-like flowers. As it grows low keep it to the front of the border. *S. chamaecyparissus* grows to about 60 cm (2 ft) while one of its hybrids, 'Nana', is lower. Pruning means trimming back after flowering. Cut hard back every few years to keep the plant bushy. Propagate by cuttings in summer.

Senecio A tough shrub, especially tolerant of wind and sea-salt breezes. However it does need a sunny-sheltered spot away from all danger of heavy frosts. The two most likely plants that you will find are *S. greyi* or *S. laxifolus*; but these are more correctly called *Senecio* 'Sunshine'. They grow to about 90 cm (3 ft) high. For pruning you simply need to tidy up any straggly branches in spring. They make an attractive informal hedge and can be propagated from cuttings in summer.

Potentilla The shrubby potentillas come in a range of yellows from lemon to gold to 'Tangerine'. They flower from summer into autumn. 'Elizabeth' is buttercup yellow. Give them a sunny position and a light, well-drained soil and they will make a rounded bush about 60 cm (2 ft) tall. Take heeled cuttings in early autumn and raise in a cold frame.

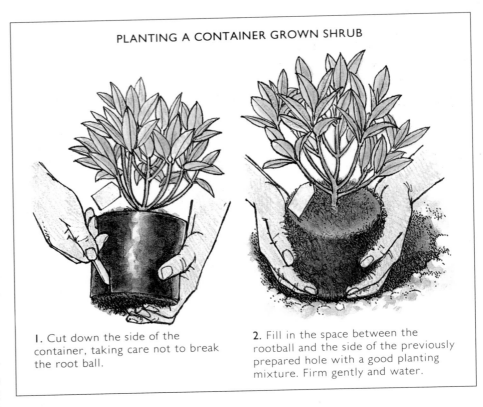

PLANTING A CONTAINER GROWN SHRUB

1. Cut down the side of the container, taking care not to break the root ball.

2. Fill in the space between the rootball and the side of the previously prepared hole with a good planting mixture. Firm gently and water.

Rhododendron (see page 37) *R. lutea* has fragrant yellow flowers; *R. wardii* has pale yellow, bell-like flowers and grows to 1.5 m (5 ft); try the evergreen hybrids 'Bo-Peep' and 'Goldsworth Yellow'.

PINK AND VIOLET FLOWERED SHRUBS

Buddleia The lovely butterfly bush grows best in a sunny, well-drained spot and deserves more care than it is usually given. Its varieties come in shades of pink and mauve, lavender and purple, growing to about 2.4 m (8 ft). Plants can easily become leggy, so hard prune back to old wood in March. 'African Queen' is deep purple; 'Black Knight' deep purple-red; 'Empire Blue' is violet-blue; 'Ile de France' rich blue-mauve; and 'Royal Red' deep pink-purple. Propagate from cuttings in the autumn.

B. alternifolia has soft purple flowers on arching branches. It will form a large dome-like shrub, up to 4.5 m (15 ft). Take heeled cuttings in late spring.

Camellia The only real problem with this beautiful shrub is that it needs to be grown in a sheltered spot, away from the wind and in lime-free soil. The more moss peat you can dig in when planting the better your camellia will grow. It likes light dappled shade. The foliage is dark glossy green and flowers in shades of pink and white appear from March to May.

Some varieties have striped petals, others double or semi-double flowers. Choose from the *C. japonica* range; 'Elegans' is pink flecked with white, 'Lady Clare' is semi-double and deep pink. *C. × williamsii* hybrids are hardier and freer flowering. 'Donation' is the most famous. Propagate from leaf cuttings – they may take many months to root.

Daphne These shrubs produce fragrant flowers in a wide range of colours from white to shades of purplish pink. *D. mezereum* is widely available and produces purplish red flowers from March to April. It grows to about 1.2 m (4 ft). *D. × burkwoodii* reaches about 90 cm (3 ft) with pink flowers, while *D. cneorum* is only about 30 cm (1 ft) tall with rose pink flowers. Daphnes need sun or a lightly shaded position and humus rich soil. Little pruning is necessary. Raise from cuttings in summer. The attractive scarlet berries are highly poisonous.

CLEMATIS

For many years now clematis has been known as the lace maker of the garden, and there is hardly a better description. Here is a plant that will clothe the ugliest fence, the barest tree stem and cover any barrier with a furnishing of flowers and foliage that are the equal of any other garden plant.

C. montana, with its masses of small white flowers in May and June will climb to any height, cascade its way over a shed or fill the wall at the front of the house. All it will ask in return is that its roots are kept in shade and its head in the sun. This is surely the great climber of the garden, although it should be stressed that it needs a little support. This may be a trellis, wires or the stem of a tree, but without some help it may well flop to the ground. It also has pink flowered forms, 'Elizabeth' and C. montana var. rubens, which are equally vigorous.

Clematis are no different from most other plants, with many different species and varieties available to choose from. There are those that will race to get head high in the sun, others that will tumble around the ground to give a mass of ground cover, and some that make free standing border plants. In flower shape too they are quite different, ranging from 'Nellie Moser' with large flat, pink petals barred with carmine red to C. viticella with its masses of small purple flowers, and C. tangutica and C. orientalis with their yellow, lantern-like flowers in late summer and autumn. The colour range runs through all the blues and the purples to white, yellow, red, pink and cream, many of these with contrasting bars.

Clematis climb quite differently from other climbers, which may rely on tendrils or sucker roots or even thorns. They hang on by their foliage stems or petioles which wrap themselves around the support and become almost tendril like. They really are at their best when climbing trees or mixed in with the branches of a shrub and can be the perfect companions to a climbing rose.

Planting and general care

Since clematis do not like being disturbed, plant them out between autumn and spring where you intend to grow them. To keep the roots moist and shaded, stones can be placed over the soil and other plants used as base cover. Tie in the young growth.

Pruning is generally dictated by the amount of space needed. If you can, allow clematis the run of its support and then leave it alone; if some pruning is needed take out old and weak stems and shorten long ones by up to a third, cutting just above a strong bud. Young plants should be pruned back to 20–23 cm (8–9 in) from the ground in early spring, but after that they will only need minimal pruning.

The following are some of the many hybrids that can be recommended:

Blue and purple 'Blue Gem' (sky blue); 'Lady Betty Balfour' (rich purple with cream stamens); 'Perle d'Azur' (pale blue); 'The President' (deep purple-blue with red stamens); and, most popular of all, 'Jackmanii Superba' (deep violet-purple).

Red 'Ernest Markham' (rich red); 'Ville de Lyon' (small and bright); 'Niobe' (ruby-red).

Pink 'Bees Jubilee' (pale pink with deeper bar); 'Hagley Hybrid' (shell pink, brown stamens); 'Nelly Moser' (pale pink with carmine red bar and at its best growing on a north facing wall).

White 'Duchess of Edinburgh'; 'Mme le Coultre (white, yellow stamens).

Clematis montana var. rubra

'Ville de Lyon'

'Nelly Moser' keeps her colour best against a north wall.

have small leaves, small clusters of tiny flowers and they need sun. The deciduous plants are hardier and with more open flowers. They can suffer damage in severe winter but there are varieties such as 'Delight', that are hardier than others. Make sure ceanothus are planted in the spring, in a warm soil and a sheltered position. If exposed to cold, wet windy weather they are in trouble right from the start. Try the deciduous 'Gloire de Versailles' with its powder blue panicles of flowers in summer and autumn and growing up to 2.1 m (7 ft). The deeper blue flowers of 'Chester' (deciduous) or the evergreen 'Autumn Blue' are also recommended. Little pruning is needed for the evergreens while the deciduous varieties require their flowered shoots to be cut back to about 90 cm (3 ft) in March. Propagate from cuttings in summer. Ideal for training against a sheltered wall or fence, or at the back of a border.

Ceratostigma The hardy plumbago is usually represented by *C. willmottianum*. It makes a very pretty shrub growing to about 90 cm (3 ft). It needs a dry, warm, sunny spot and thrives on chalky soil with its bright blue flowers appearing late in summer and autumn. It makes a delightful partner for Michaelmas daisies. Pruning means cutting back to about ground level every April. Propagation is by division of roots or summer cuttings.

Hebe Once known as veronica, these come in many shapes and sizes, and colours too, so decide where you are going to plant it before making your purchase. For the blue border the violet-blue flowers of 'Autumn Glory' are a dominating brilliance from June to November and are accompanied by evergreen foliage of green and purple. 'Veitchii' is bright blue, 'Midsummer Beauty' lavender, but there are many others to choose from in shades of mauve, pink, lavender and white. The shiny foliage of these bushy plants make them a great attraction in the garden but remember that they can be tender especially in very cold areas. Very little pruning is needed and they will easily strike from short sideshoots taken in summer.

Hydrangea (see page 42)

Left: *Hebe* 'Midsummer Beauty' is evergreen, like all hebes, and suitable for seaside planting.

Opposite: Wisteria in full flower is one of the loveliest sights in early summer.

Lavandula For a fragrant edging that flowers between mid summer and early autumn, lavender is unsurpassed. *L. vera* is pale blue. While *L. spica* is the old English lavender. They like a limy soil, well drained, and good sun. Take away flowers as they fade (they are used the world over for pot-pourri) and then trim back in March. Do not cut into the hard wood when pruning. Summer cuttings will provide new plants.

Rhododendron (see page 37) 'Blue Tit' grows to about 90 cm (3 ft) and is lavender blue. Suitable for the rock garden.

Syringa Lilac is one of the most prolific shrubs and is found in many gardens where it forms a graceful small tree. You may think of it clothed in fragrant trusses of lilac or purple flowers but there is a special beauty in those lovely white cultivars. Unfortunately the flowering period lasts only a few short weeks early in summer. Lilacs do well in most soils and only need pruning after flowering when any thin unproductive wood should be cut away. 'Charles Joly' has double purple flowers; 'Souvenir de Louis Spaeth' is single and purple, and *S. velutina* has mauve flowers and forms an attractive rounded bush reaching 1.8 m (6 ft). Generally speaking all cultivars are grafted so propagation is not recommended, however some of the species can be grown from heeled cuttings taken in summer.

Wisteria Lilac-blue flowers hang in long trusses in May and June. This vigorous climber can top 6 m (20 ft). It looks at its best trained over a pergola or against a sunny wall in a humus-rich soil. Cut back side shoots in summer and long growths in winter. It is propagated from eye cuttings, small pieces of stem containing a bud. These are pressed into a pot containing a peat/sand mixture. Cover with clingfilm until signs of growth show.

WHITE FLOWERED SHRUBS

Buddleia (see page 40) 'White Cloud' and 'White Bouquet', both hybrids of *B. davidii*, are ideal for the white garden.

Camellia (see page 40) The single white *C. japonica* 'Alba Simplex' is to be highly recommended.

Carpenteria Fragrant white flowers appear in mid summer. This shrub needs to be given full sun and as frost free a situation as possible. It will grow tall, up to 3 m (10 ft). Choose *C. californica* 'Ladham's Variety' which needs tipping back and a light pruning in spring. Propagate from cuttings in summer.

Chaenomeles (see page 37) 'Nivalis' is a fine white variety of *C. speciosa*.

Choisya The Mexican orange blossom is one of the neatest of garden shrubs forming a dome of glossy green trifoliate evergreen leaves. Only one species is available – *C. ternata* – and this grows to about 1.8 m (6 ft) over a period of six years. The flowers that are produced in May resemble orange blossom and the leaves

Carpenteria californica needs a sheltered spot and is best grown against a south- or west-facing wall.

Left: Mexican orange blossom (*Choisya ternata*) has attractive evergreen foliage.

Opposite: Lucky white heather, *Erica herbacea* 'Springwood White', providing attractive ground cover with ivy.

when crushed are fragrant. Plant in a sunny position or in partial shade in a well-drained, even a chalky soil. It needs little pruning but may be damaged by frost, in which case any dead or damaged wood should be cut out. Propagate from cuttings in summer; these should root with ease.

Cotoneaster These range from low ground-hugging plants to elegant trees, but all have small white flowers, often tinged with pink in June. One of the most popular is the wall-hugging *C. horizontalis* which grows from 60 cm to 1.2 m (2 to 4 ft). Often called the fishbone cotoneaster because of its distinctive branching pattern, it is deciduous with showy red berries in autumn. For orange berries try the graceful *C. franchetti; C.* 'Rothschildianus' has yellow berries and both will grow to 1.8 m

(6 ft). Cotoneasters grow well in most soils but prefer a sunny position. Trim back into shape in spring if necessary.

Deutzia (see page 41) The excellent white *D. scabra* 'Plena' carries double white flowers which are light purple on the reverse of the petals.

Erica (see page 41) Everyone wants to grow lucky white heather. 'Springwood White' is low growing, reliable, and quite the best white variety. It flowers in winter.

Hydrangea (see page 42) *H. paniculata* 'Grandiflora' carries large heads of white flowers in late summer, turning pink with age. A spreading shrub reaching 1.5 m (5 ft). 'Lanarth White' is a lacecap from the *H. macrophylla* group.

Magnolia Not quite as difficult to grow as many believe. It does need a little tender, loving care in both planting and in the selection of a well dug, humus-rich, sunny site. A moisture-retentive soil is essential and to this end place plenty of good rotted compost around the roots and as a mulch. There are some magnolias which eventually form trees like *M. grandiflora* which is most spectacular and grows to 6m (20 ft) with large flowers from July to the end of September.

'Alba Superba' is one of the popular *M. × soulangiana* hybrids and grows to about 3 m (10 ft) high, while *M. stellata* is bush like and only half that size with dainty, star-like flowers in March and April. *M. × highdownensis* is a beautiful hybrid of the purest white which flowers late in spring.

Rhododendron (see page 37) 'Sappho' is a beautiful white-flowered hardy hybrid, but may grow over 4 m (13 ft) high.

Romneya The tree poppy grows to 1.8 m (6 ft) high. Large white fragrant flowers with a yellow eye are borne from July to October on *R. coulteri* or until the first frost kills them. Frost may kill the plant back too but it usually grows again well enough in spring. Give it full sun, some shelter and a warm soil. It rarely survives transplanting. In March prune it to within a few centimetres of the ground. Propagate by cutting the thick roots into pieces and planting them, right way up, in a pot containing a peat/sand mixture.

Romneya coulteri, the tree poppy.

Rosa (see pages 51 to 63)

Olearia (the daisy bush) Huge heads of white daisies appear on *O. × haastii* between July and September. This evergreen bush grows to 1.8 m (6 ft). It needs sunshine and a well-drained soil. Although it cannot stand frost it copes well with wind. Remove faded blooms after flowering and then prune out any dead or damaged shoots in April. If it grows too tall it can be kept down by hard pruning after flowering. Propagate from cuttings in summer.

Philadelphus The mock orange forms an elegant shrub covered with very fragrant white flowers in June or July. 'Belle Etoile' is a wonderful single-flowered shrub and 'Manteau d'Hermine' has

double flowers; these are just two of many good cultivars there are to choose from. They grow to just over 1.8 m (6 ft) in most garden soils and like a sunny position or one of light shade. Propagate from hardwood cuttings in autumn.

Pyracantha The firethorn is best known for its masses of red berries in autumn and winter. In cold spells, these provide a popular source of food for birds. However this spiny, evergreen shrub also is smothered in tiny white flowers early in summer. It is generally grown as a wall shrub but it can be used within a border where it can reach to 1.8 m (6 ft) high. Prune back unwanted shoots. Propagate from seed or from summer cuttings.

Spiraea Easy to grow and quick to establish. There are several different types to choose from. The spring flowering ones

Philadelphus, mock orange, brings fragrance to the garden in summer.

Spiraea × arguta in full flower lives up to its familiar name of bridal wreath.

47

The spreading branches of *Viburnum plicatum* 'Mariesii' bear masses of flower heads in early summer.

generally produce white flowers. They are carried in many different ways – spikes, domes and even flat heads. The pure white heads of *Spiraea × arguta*, also known as bridal wreath or foam of May, are a wonderful sight. This shrub grows to about 1.8 m (6 ft).

Summer flowering spiraeas tend to be pink to purple. For something really unusual, try *S. japonica* 'Shirobana', 60 cm (2 ft) high, with a mixture of deep pink, crimson and white flowers during the summer months. These deciduous shrubs prefer a sunny position and a humus-rich soil. They can be raised in a frame from cuttings taken in summer.

Syringa (lilac – see page 44)   'Madame Lemoine' has glorious panicles of double white flowers.

Viburnum   A varied group of shrubs with white or pink-tinged flowers; several also have attractive berries late in the year. *V. × carlesii* is a rounded shrub with fragrant white flowers in spring. It grows to about 1.5 m (5 ft). *V. plicatum* 'Mariesii' has large flat flowerheads. *V. farreri* carries sweet scented flowers in winter on bare branches. *V. opulus* 'Sterile' is known as the snowball tree because of its huge balls of sterile florets carried in summer; its foliage colours well in autumn too. The evergreen *V. tinus* is greatly under-rated. This winter flowering shrub makes an excellent hedge and provides a fine background for spring-flowering bulbs. Viburnums need little in the way of pruning and most can be propagated from cuttings taken in summer and raised in a heated propagating frame.

Weigela (see page 37)   'Mont Blanc' has fragrant white flowers. Another good white variety is *W. florida* 'Alba'.

PLANT CARE

Even the best planned and best planted garden can be taken over completely by nature in a matter of months if left uncared for. But such care does not necessarily mean hard work, but it does mean keeping a constant lookout for aphids, caterpillars, emerging weeds, flowers that have died off, and those that are suffering from lack of water. On pages 89 to 92 we look in detail at the pests and diseases that you have to watch out for, so here I shall concentrate on some of the remaining key things you have to do to keep your garden in top notch.

Viburnum farreri is winter flowering.

Watering

Before starting any planting session you must water the soil, and thereafter ensure your plant or shrub does not dry out and wilt. Even in what seems a wet season there are often plants in a closely planted bed or border that will get very little rain simply because the larger foliage is acting as an umbrella, so never assume that nature has given your plants sufficient water. Keep a close eye on them through the year, but never going to the opposite extreme of keeping your beds soaking wet all the time. Also, every plant needs time to absorb the water in the soil so you must allow for a drying-out spell.

When you bed-out new plants they will need to be well watered immediately (it is best if the soil is already wet). For the following few weeks, until they have become established, they will most likely need more watering, especially if there is a dry period in spring or early summer. When they become established they will be quite happy to go for longer periods without watering, but in drought conditions or in a period of warm, windy weather they will need attention. As soon as the top couple of inches of soil becomes dry or the foliage begins to look dull, that is the time to water.

Also ensure that you water thoroughly. A dribble around each plant does more harm than good. Ideally use a hose to water the immediate root area until it is well soaked, and then move on to the next plant.

A watering can is quite effective in a small area, but the constant filling can make it a terrible chore.

Feeding

All plants will suffer hunger pangs and look 'demoralized' if they are not occasionally fed. Although different plants have different feeding patterns, so often in a garden the miniature plants get the same amount as the large, hungrier ones, with the result that the little ones are over-fed and the large plants are left at almost starvation point. (There are a few plants that grow better if they are left without food, but they are so few that they need not concern us here.)

Feeding begins when a planting spot is being prepared. The inclusion of bone meal or a general fertilizer is vital to get the plant off to a good start. After that a fertilizer can be sprinkled around the roots, while a soluble or liquid fertilizer is very effective for the large leafed plants. The purpose of feeding is to build up a plant's resources, as much as to help it to give its best immediately, and for this reason annuals do not need feeding to the same extent as perennials.

Remember that all powder or granular fertilizers should be used only when the ground is moist, that they should be kept off foliage and away from the stems. After spreading they should be raked into the top couple of inches of soil. Foliar feeding is a very acceptable method of fertilizing, especially when you want instant results, for example when a plant needs to recover from an insect or disease attack, or after a particularly wet or windy spell when the plant has been under stress. A dilutor or hoser on the end of a hose pipe will do the job effectively and quickly.

Hoeing and weeding

Weeds may look lovely in the countryside but they rarely enhance anyone's garden. Indeed, if they are given the freedom to grow then they can undo all the good work you have put into your garden. They compete for space, food, water, look unsightly, and eventually take over the whole area.

The best way to keep them down is with

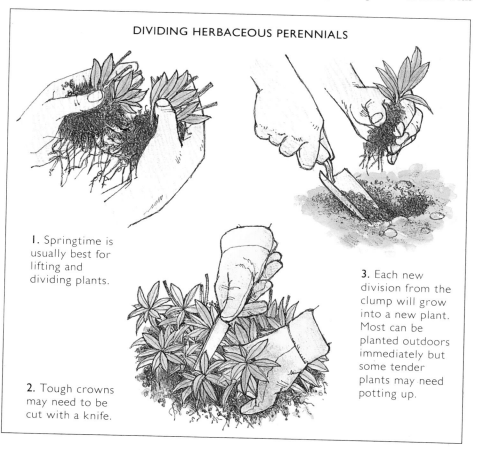

DIVIDING HERBACEOUS PERENNIALS

1. Springtime is usually best for lifting and dividing plants.

2. Tough crowns may need to be cut with a knife.

3. Each new division from the clump will grow into a new plant. Most can be planted outdoors immediately but some tender plants may need potting up.

a hoe. Regular hoeing as soon as seedling weeds appear should ensure control. However, if you do intend to use a chemical please follow the rules on the label precisely and keep it safely locked away. Never leave any trace of a weedkiller in a container that a child might drink from. If you do use a watering can for a weedkiller, label it, and do not use it again for any other gardening task.

Many weed problems will be stopped at source if roots and pieces of root are removed. But it does not matter how thorough you have been, some will reappear from time to time. Hoeing these weeds when they are tiny and before they get a chance to reseed the ground is vital. Hoe gently and with care, never going any deeper than is absolutely necessary. If there are any deep-rooted weeds, such as dandelion, dock, nettle or thistle, dig them out by hand.

Staking

Staking in a garden can often look ugly, but it is necessary for many plants that are weak stemmed or for tall ones that are growing on exposed sites. There is nothing worse than finding plants that have been caught by an overnight wind and damaged, almost beyond repair.

Once you know the plants that need staking – those that are tall, large-headed, spindly or climbers – then you can tie them while they are still quite small. There is no point waiting until the weather becomes windy, for once a plant has collapsed, perhaps from its own weight, it will never recover, cannot be repaired and will only be fit for the compost heap.

For most plants ordinary pea sticks will suffice – just push them into the soil when the plant is about 30 cm (12 in) tall. With plants that need higher staking use bamboo canes, but don't clump too many stems together. Instead, set three or four canes about 23 cm (9 in) apart, at the corners of an imaginary triangle or square. Tie gardening string round the canes, creating a 'cage'. This holds in the plants but also gives them some freedom, and plenty of air and light. With some specialist plants like dahlias, chrysanthemums, sweet pea or standard roses, the stakes should be put in before planting so as not to damage the roots or tubers, in the case of dahlias, in any way.

STAKING

1. Many plants need support, especially in the herbaceous border. Put stakes in early. Place three or four canes around the stems, keeping growth tidy by means of string tied around the canes.

2. Smaller plants can be easily kept in place with small twiggy sticks. Do not just tie stems to a single cane.

Pruning and cutting back

There is surprisingly little pruning or cutting back needed in the flower garden. The removal of spent blooms in the summer or cutting back of growth when a plant becomes overcrowded, is all that is involved. Among the spring-flowering plants in the rockery many will put out ugly foliage in the summer, and this can be cut back without affecting the plant – often some cutting back will bring the bonus of a second set of flowers.

The same message applies to winter and spring pruning. The majority of plants die down by themselves. Annuals will, of course, die off; the remnants can go on the compost heap. The only other job for the gardener is to cut down and clear away the dead foliage and begin to make plans for the following year's flowers. There may be some plants such as border roses, which will need pruning, and this is dealt with later in the book. Many fuchsias die back naturally – if they don't they can be hard pruned right to the ground, but not before March. However, if you live in a very mild area you may find that fuchsias retain their foliage right through the winter.

Winter tasks

For a great number of plants winter means rest, but there are some, like the half-hardy perennials, that will need lifting and storing until it is time for planting again in the spring. If you wish to take a chance you could leave the plants in the ground, covering the crowns with peat moss, twigs, and leafmould to keep them frost free, until the following spring. But, having said that, it should be added that the gardener ought to make his own investigations about his plants so that their winter care requirements are known. Evergreens and winter-flowering plants should, of course, be left alone.

A very light dig with a fork is all that is needed to clear up the beds and borders, which also gives you a chance to take out any perennial weeds that have escaped attention earlier in the year. It should be stressed that this is a careful operation, and that roots should not be disturbed unless a plant is to be lifted and divided. If you have delicate alpines they will need protection from the rain. You can either construct a small plastic housing, or cover them with a sheet of glass.

THE ROSE GARDEN

Since medieval times the rose has been called the flower of flowers. And it still reigns supreme as the most adaptable of plants, a symbol of absolute beauty, purity, peace and joy. Undoubtedly a great deal of its popularity has been built on a certain mystique, but this is allied to the fact that the rose can be grown just about anywhere, in a mixed border, its own special bed, in rockeries and on large banks, in containers, and window boxes, and in warm greenhouses and conservatories.

There is hardly a large or small, public or private garden in Great Britain today without a rose of some kind. And every year more and more new rose varieties are being developed to add to the thousands already on sale, increasing the range of colours, fragrances, shapes and styles. Many of the new varieties echo the old roses, but bring with them the best of the modern varieties. Miniature roses, which really only became popular 50 years ago, are now almost a cult on their own. Today there are so many roses for every type of garden, and for every position within these gardens, that it is no wonder new gardeners are bewildered by the enormity of the choice.

The nature of the rose has changed in just over a century. Before the late 1800s it was expected to flower for only a short time in the early summer months but, even for this period, the beauty of the rose was such that it would have been churlish to have expected more from the Damasks, Musks Bourbons, Albas, and others. Today, with the arrival of hybrid teas (large flowered), floribundas (cluster flowered), miniatures and climbers, that provide flowers from May until December, the rose has had adaptability allied to old fashioned beauty.

Rose lovers now find that even the smallest garden can be turned into a true rose garden with plants that are scaled-down versions of the delightful old style varieties. If you prefer the older roses, then provided you have a medium size garden there shouldn't be any problem. When deciding which kind of rose to buy, also consider the most recent innovations, the English roses, which bring together the flowers of the old roses with the almost constant flowering possibilities of modern varieties. Finally, there are the patio roses, small and compact, with medium sized flowers, being far more versatile than the name suggests.

It's very tempting, when deciding where to plant a rose, to give it too much prominence. Instead, you should consider mixing them. So a yellow climber such as 'Golden Showers', or a shrub such as 'Mountbatten' will excel when interlaced with the blue *Clematis* 'Countess of Lovelace' or 'Perle d'Azur'. Roses really mix superbly well with herbaceous flowers, although many people believe this is sacrilege. To prove the point, just imagine a border with roses mixed with hollyhocks, delphiniums, foxgloves and a carpet of pinks at their feet. Nor are violas, and the grey tints of catmint and lavender, Canterbury bells (*Campanula*) and perlargoniums out of place with the rose. Similarly,

Hybrid tea rose 'Just Joey' has ruffled petals and superb colour.

in shrub borders, the rose is invaluable and mixes well with forsythia, lilac and flowering currants (*Ribes*).

Underplanting, other than in mixed borders, can be a problem when the rose bed needs mulching and feeding, the process being hindered by the presence of other smaller plants. But that does not apply to spring bulbs, while violas, primulas and auriculas, if used with care, can be a lovely foil. In all cases the shrubs, perennials and low-growing plants and bulbs can bring colour to the garden when the rose is out of flower, and at other times will create an exciting foreground or backdrop, as with delphiniums which make ideal bed-mates for roses.

HYBRID TEAS

Probably the ultimate in the rose breeder's skills is shown in the hybrid teas (also described as large-flowered bush roses) that produce the largest and most beautifully formed blooms of all. The colour range only lacks the true blue and the deep black. They are also the most highly scented group of the modern roses, but their greatest glory comes from their ability to produce continuous crops of flowers from early summer to mid-winter.

Where they are grown in the garden is best decided by you. Ignore such advice that demands hybrid teas are grown in beds of one type. Siting the rose is an artistic decision, partly influenced by the shape, height and colour of its companion plants. You should have few problems in making a decision, particularly when planting such splendid roses as the lovely big 'Solitaire' with its yellow touched red blooms, the copper of 'Just Joey', the soft apricot of 'Helen Traubel', the red and almost cabbage sized 'Alec's Red', and the yellow-pink and orange of 'Lincoln Cathedral'. They all have their place when well-grown, and will show they are robust enough to grow in a group of their own or among the plants in a mixed border.

Every year hybrid teas are improved. In recent times the greatest changes have been brought by the Scottish-bred 'Silver Jubilee' (a soft confection of pink and cream) which has passed on its great foliage, well-shaped blooms and good, even bush growth to many new varieties. Another recent rose, the vermillion, tall-growing 'Alexander', is also the herald of strong growth and flower power in tomorrow's roses.

Among the hybrid teas there are many cultivars which are grown only by exhibitors who are prepared to cover them so that rain does not harm the blooms. Unfortunately many of these roses find their way into the ordinary garden because they have been seen in full beauty at a flower show and assumed to be a typical rose. The best place for the non-exhibitor to see roses is therefore in a garden or a rose grower's field. Tempting though it is to buy roses on the basis of reading a marvellous description, you should remember that nothing beats seeing roses 'in the flesh', when you will instinctively know whether they are your kind of flowers and which varieties you prefer.

FLORIBUNDAS

It always seems much easier to place floribundas in mixed borders and beds because of the clusters of blooms that they carry, with an informality that is often lacking among the hybrid teas. It is this characteristic which gives them their alternative classification as cluster-flowered bush roses. Unfortunately the floribundas are not the greatest possessors of fragrance, although a little searching will reveal that there are quite a number of pleasantly scented varieties available, including 'Margaret Merril', 'English Miss', 'Arthur Bell', 'Korresia', and 'Fragrant Delight'.

Floribundas can be seen at their best in beds of one variety, but this should not stop anyone using them with groups of other plants. The flower type is extremely varied, ranging from the hybrid tea perfection of shape, to the old fashioned quartered and loose petalled flowers. The colour range is also extremely wide, with some beautiful types of blooms that have not been repeated as successfully in the hybrid teas. The mauves, purples and lilacs are very well represented, with superb cultivars such as 'Escapade' (light lilac) the much deeper 'Lilac Charm', and the beetroot-purple 'News'. The distinctive pink of 'Elizabeth of Glamis' is matched with a lovely fragrance, but this one can be difficult to grow, not always being sufficiently hardy in a severe winter. And one of the most famous floribundas is 'Queen Elizabeth', justly revered for its enormous quantities of blooms. It is also tough, and does not demand much attention other than heavy pruning in the spring.

The range of floribundas available to British gardeners is second to none, and the type of roses available is extraordinary. There are even some excellent low growers, including the scented 'Amber Queen', 'Korresia (the best of the yellows), 'Trumpeter' (the best of the reds), the white 'Iceberg', and the lovely pink, 'Sexy Rexy' (which will triumph despite, or possibly because of its name).

SHRUBS

The way roses are being bred today you could grow just about any rose as a shrub whether it be a hybrid tea, floribunda or an old garden rose. However, there is a special classification for shrubs, which is broken down between old and modern varieties. They embrace a huge range of roses some of which grow like climbers, others that need huge spaces, and some that flower right through from spring to late autumn. They also have a wide range of flowers, from those with five petals, to others numbering almost 100. In bush form, some are lax and others upright; some will make an enormous bush, while others stay well within the normal range of 60 cm–1.2 m (2 ft–4 ft) high. Such a diversity should immediately convey the old but still highly valid message 'Let the buyer beware', because no matter how pretty the sales pictures and descriptions may be, one of your first considerations must be select a rose for the space you have available.

Choosing a shrub is obviously a very personal matter, but I feel that the new English roses will prove to be very popular. They are a mixture of the old roses and the newer types, and combine flowers in the form and in the style of old roses (mostly big, heavy-petalled, and perfumed) with the repeat flowering of the modern varieties. They are available in wonderful colours, though the bush form may still need a little improvement. Nonetheless, it is a fine addition for the borders.

Placing shrubs at the back of the border will give a great framework and a long-flowering period, from a form that blends easily with the herbaceous and perennials.

The rose garden at
the Royal
Horticultural
Society's Garden at
Wisley in Surrey.

Left: 'Ballerina' is a delightful shrub rose suitable for growing in a tub as well as in the open garden.

Opposite: The deservedly popular miniature rose 'Baby Masquerade'.

But do make sure that the size is what you want. When it comes to colour you will find few yellows among the old roses, but two new ones – 'Graham Thomas' from the English roses, and 'Mountbatten' – are worth seeking out. They ensure there's no excuse for omitting a shrub rose from your garden, whether it be large or small.

MINIATURES

These roses are usually half the size (or even smaller) of those already mentioned, and twice the value. They can be grown in the front of a border, in a pocket of a rockery, or along the top of a wall or bank that has sufficient soil. They are also ideal for window boxes, tubs, the greenhouse, and even the conservatory. In fact they are the most versatile of all small plants. And the colour range too is everything you could ask for, ranging from lavender to green, from whites to pure reds, and from pink to apricot, with others in bicolors. Miniatures are so popular that in some parts of the world they sell in greater numbers than all the other types of roses combined. Yet 10 years ago they were widely being dismissed as 'toy roses'.

What exactly is a miniature rose? To most people it is a small plant, no more than about 30 cm (12 in) high, with small flowers and small foliage. But that isn't necessarily so, for miniatures today come in sizes varying from 7.5–10 cm (3–4 in) high, to shrubs and climbers which grow to 1.2–1.5 m (4–5 ft) high carrying masses of tiny blooms. But bloom size too can vary, from the very small to about 4 cm (1½ in) across when fully open.

The world's number one miniature has existed since the 1960s. It is the French-bred orange-red called 'Starina' that carries perfectly shaped blooms on a well-shaped bush. But it is now being closely rivalled by the newer varieties. My own nomination as the best of the miniatures for garden growing is the coral-pink 'Angela Rippon', which is widely available.

Most of the top new miniatures have been bred in America where there is an astonishing boom in their sales, though they are only now beginning to arrive in Great Britain. However, widely available throughout the country are small potted roses ('Sunblaze' and 'Rosamini' are but two) from French and Dutch breeders. These are generally sold in flower, and once they have bloomed in the house they can be transferred to the garden. Indeed, these purchases can often prove very good value for the pots generally have three or four little plants that have been struck from cuttings, which can be separated and planted out individually in the garden or into pots or a window box.

One of the great benefits of the miniatures is that they are very simple to grow from cuttings. In fact, one American writer says that they grow so easily from cuttings that 'they spread like gossip'. Certainly they are easy to propagate and very easy to fall in love with. An additional bonus of taking these cuttings is that the plants will often be far more dainty than those that have been produced by the more traditional method of budding or grafting.

CLIMBERS AND RAMBLERS

Calling roses ramblers and climbers is, in a way, giving a false impression because they will not climb or ramble without some help from the gardener or from nature by way of support. This support may have to be wires, tying, or help to find a way through an old tree. Once that help is provided, and if you have objects to cover, such as an archway or tree stump, then the results should be spectacular.

Ramblers and climbers are quite distinct. The ramblers have been with us for

generations, their huge trusses carrying hundreds of generally small blooms. They provide a mass of colour all through the summer, but there is only one flush of blooms. Their main use nowadays is where a rampant grower is needed to provide colour and foliage high up in old trees. But later they can be quite troublesome, needing attention if their condition deteriorates, and cutting back after their summer flowering. Among the best of them are 'Albertine' (pale pink and very fragrant), 'American Pillar' (deep pink, white eye), and 'Crimson Shower' (crimson with a light fragrance), while the giant and tree topping *Rosa filipes* 'Kiftsgate' will cover anything where it can grow rampantly and without hindrance.

Climbers are quite a different proposition. Their stems are stiff, with flowers ranging from the small to those as large as on the hybrid teas. Many are also tough and fairly disease resistant, while new ones are being hybridized all the time. The latter have the added bonus of being repeat flowering – for perfection look to 'Handel',

An archway wreathed in roses.

Rosa filipes
'Kiftsgate' will cover the branches of the tallest tree; give it plenty of space.

'Albertine' is one of the most popular and vigorous of the ramblers. Its copper-pink buds open early in summer.

which has cream with rosy-pink edgings to the flower, the apricot-pink 'Compassion', or the deep red 'Dublin Bay'. In one respect these modern climbers are quite different to the older ones, like some of the climbing Bourbons (such as the lovely 'Zephirine Drouhin') because they do not grow with the same vigour – some will only reach 3 m (10 ft) high, and only then after quite a struggle.

Also widely available are climbing versions (called sports) of many bush roses. Unfortunately these climbing roses usually put all their energy into producing the first batch of flowers, which means that you get very little of the repeat flowering benefits of the bush form. But when they bloom they can be spectacular, with 'Cl. Shot Silk', 'Cl. Mrs Sam McGredy' and 'Cl. Ena Harkness' being among the best available.

More than any other group of roses the climbers need careful choosing. Check their potential for repeat flowering, their expected height, size of flower, fragrance, and disease resistance before purchase.

BUYING

The best time to see roses and to make your selection is during the summer when the full effects of weathering can be seen on the blooms. Roses make wonderful pictures in catalogues, but the compilers often fail to show or mention the growth habit, the amount of thorns, the real colour, the height, whether it is bushy, upright, open, or spreading, and the amount of rain resistance there is in the flower. The ideal bedding roses, in my opinion, are 'Silver Jubilee' (peachy cream), 'Trumpeter' (orange-red), 'Korresia' (yellow), 'The Times' (dark red), 'Just Joey' (fragrant, coppery orange) and 'Iceberg' (white), but there are hundreds of others that are worth considering.

The sooner you order in the summer the better your chance of getting top-class bushes. The roses will generally be sent to you bare-rooted from November onwards. Huge numbers of gardeners also buy prepackaged roses which are bare rooted but they may suffer by having only a little peat moss or compost around the roots to keep them moist. You can also buy container grown roses, which are the ideal kind to plant during the growing season.

With all these roses you are looking for a good strong bush that looks healthy. Anything less is not worth buying – there is no such thing as a bargain rose. Stems should be green and without the wrinkles that point to wilting, and they should be well ripened (most bronze type foliage or stems will be unripe). There should be, at the very least, two good stems, and the roots system should have some fibrous growth. The buds should be dormant in all prepackaged and bare root purchases.

PLANNING

There are no rules as to where you should plant a rose or how they should be planted. Although it is advantageous to remember that beds are better planted with only one kind, and that borders can be multipurpose, these rules can be ignored if the roses are properly placed within their confines. There is nothing worse than a huge bed or front garden of roses thrown together like a handful of smarties – different colours but no overall shape. While I do not believe that plant colours ever clash, I do feel that some control is needed. Without it you will have a chaotic mass of tall stems and buried blooms entangled in an unsightly mess. Another general point worth considering is that hybrid teas are best kept in a batch on their own where the individual blooms can be admired, while floribundas are the roses for big splashes of colour.

Key planning points
- With bedding roses plant the taller varieties in the centre.
- Stagger the planting within a bed.
- Keep the roses at least 45 cm (18 in) from the outside edges of the beds to avoid problems when trimming the grass.
- Don't make the bed any deeper than 1.5 m (5 ft), otherwise you will have difficulty reaching and cutting off dead heads.
- The same points apply to borders and to beds, except that as the roses are not being seen from all sides the tallest (like 'Queen Elizabeth' and 'Alexander') should be at the back, medium-sized growers in the centre, and low growers (such as the miniatures and the patios) in the front row.
- Try to plant roses in batches of three to five to form a group of one colour.
- Some roses make good hedges, but do check the height and colour before you place your order. There is a huge range of roses available in this category, providing a superb all the year round flowering screen to just about any height.
- There are many roses, such as the new patio types 'Sweet Dreams', 'Sweet Magic' and 'Cider Cup', and the older 'Ballerina' with its five petalled blooms of light pink and white eye which are ideal for planting in tubs and urns.

PLANTING

There is no such thing as a successful, shaded rose garden. The rose, even more than other flowers, needs sunshine galore as well as plenty of water, food, air and light. It is improved by being sheltered from cold winds.

The planting time lasts from late October to late March. There is no doubt that the sooner you can get the bushes in the ground the better chance they have of settling down quickly, and the better their growth and flowering will be during their first season.

Most of what has been said about soil for flowers also applies to roses. The best kind is a medium loam that isn't water-logged, and which has a pH of around 6.5. However if your soil needs attention, then use peat to increase acidity, and nitrochalk to increase alkalinity. The finest thing you can do for the rose bed is to add manure or other humus. You should prepare the soil so that there will be time for it to settle before the arrival of the bushes. When the bushes do arrive, waste no time in planting them. With bare root or root-wrapped roses it is better to get them heeled into the ground in a protected spot if the soil is unsuitable for planting. This involves covering the roots and lower parts of the stems with soil, and leaving them until conditions have improved.

When you unpack your roses, whether they be in a grower's bag or are pre-packaged from the store, place them into a full bucket of water and give them a good soaking. Then cut away all the broken, decayed or spindly shoots, and cut back any very long shoots to about 30 cm (1 ft) from the base. The next task involves creating the planting mixture in a wheelbarrow. Use one part soil, one part moist peat, and four (gloved) handfulls of bone meal. Mix thoroughly.

Once a good size hole has been dug, spread out the roots in it, particularly if they are all growing in one direction. Now cover the roots with the planting mix, keeping the bud union (the knot-like portion where the roots meet the top growth) about 2–3 cm (1 in) below the soil level.

Use the same technique to transplant older roses, but note that it will require more watering. You should also beware of planting new bushes in soil where roses have been previously grown. They will not thrive. If you must use the same place then make sure that you remove an area at least 60 × 60 cm (2 × 2 ft).

PRUNING

Nothing frightens the new gardener more than the thought of pruning, yet it is quite a simple task, once you know the rules. They involve:

- Pruning from mid March in the south of the country, to early April in the north. Pruning too early means that premature growth can be killed off by winter frosts. Pruning too late means that a lot of important early growth is wasted.
- Using the best secateurs. They are costly but definitely worth the extra money. No matter what kind you use, make sure they are always kept clean and sharp.
- Trimming back long growth to about half the length of the stem. Follow this by cutting out entirely all dead wood and any stems that are diseased or damaged. If the pith is not pure white keep cutting until it is; this is the sign of healthy growth.
- Cutting out all thin stems and those that rub against each other. Unripe growth must also be removed.
- Producing a clean, ripe, strong and healthy bush with an open centre.

PLANTING A ROSE BUSH

1. Fit and spread the roots snugly into the hole after pruning the rose.

2. Replace the soil and firm in gently with the foot.

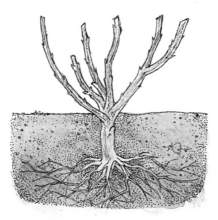

3. The bud union should be slightly below ground level when planted so that it will level off as soil settles. Insert label in the soil by the bush.

PRUNING A ROSE

1. First remove old, dead or broken wood.

2. Take out all twiggy growth and thin out the centre of the bush.

3. Hybrid teas may be pruned hard to five or six eyes from the base but bushes should be pruned to suit the garden.

Note: Ramblers are pruned in late summer or autumn as soon as flowering has finished.

Climbers need little pruning, but do cut away any old, damaged wood, and leave the climber at the length and height and spread dictated by the needs of its position and your garden.

GENERAL MAINTENANCE

This involves three principal tasks:

Mulching This operation keeps the ground moist, eliminates many weeds, and improves the soil structure. If manure is used it provides some food for the roses.

Watering Roses need more water than most plants, but that does not mean that they like to be kept standing in mud. Young and newly planted or transplanted bushes need water regularly in a dry spell. A little soluble fertilizer in the water never does any harm. Roses can take up to 9.1 lt (2 gl) each, every couple of days.

Feeding A small handfull of fertilizer should be applied to every bush in the spring when the soil is moist. If this is repeated every month until the end of July there will be a wonderful response from the plant. Foliar feeding is also very useful – wet the leaves thoroughly and spray using a diluter or hoser on the end of a hosepipe.

PROBLEMS

It is not possible to eliminate all the troubles from a rose garden, but by tackling problems before they appear the gardener should always be the winner. The major problems are three diseases known as **black spot, mildew** and **rust**, all of which live up to their names and are easy to spot.

Spray with a recommended fungicide immediately after pruning, so that any left-over spores are eliminated. After that, spray once a month to prevent these diseases from taking hold. Most chemical treatments are designed to prevent rather than cure, although some of the newer ones do have curative qualities.

When spraying, follow these tips. Do not spray in sunny or windy weather, but when the foliage is dry, preferably in the evening. Spray the top and bottom of the foliage until the liquid drips from it. You should wear clothes that cover and protect as much of your skin as possible. Also wear a mask and glasses. And finally, once you have finished, throw away empty chemical containers into the rubbish bin, and drain away any left over solution.

Other problems caused by aphids and the like should be handled individually. It is useless spraying with a multichemical if there is no need for an insecticide. However, when aphids do appear then a cocktail spray that includes an insecticide, fungicide and some foliar feeding is perfect for the roses.

Regular spraying against all bugs and these specific diseases will pay off, and even if you have only a couple of bushes far greater results will be achieved by constant care and attention. You should also watch out for caterpillars, slugworms, beatles, and so on.

RECOMMENDED VARIETIES

This list contains a number of roses of proven ability which will go on flowering with normal care and attention for 15 to 20 years – and maybe longer.

HYBRID TEAS

'Alec's Red' Crimson, globular and very fragrant. Vigorous growth. Needs watching for black spot.

'Alexander' Vermillion, medium sized with a slight fragrance. Brilliant colouring and a tall grower. Cut flowers when they are young.

'Blessings' Coral pink, medium sized, fragrant. The ideal bedding rose with wonderful flower producing abilities. (See page 60.)

'Double Delight' Creamy white, edged raspberry red, large and very fragrant. Exquisite in a warm, sunny, dry summer, but falls victim to mildew easily. Blooms also 'ball' in the rain.

'Fragrant Cloud' Geranium red, large, very fragrant. Excellent for bedding but does need watching for signs of mildew and rust.

'Grandpa Dickson' Lemon yellow, large, slightly fragrant. An upright grower, needing to be well fed and watered to get it to its best.

'Harry Wheatcroft' Scarlet, striped yellow, large, slight fragrance. Flamboyant and named after one of the rose world's greatest characters.

'Helen Traubel' Apricot, large and fragrant. A lovely rose that blooms heavily but often has weak stems. Waterproof.

Hybrid tea 'Blessings' is ideal for bedding with its splendid flower producing abilities.

'**Just Joey**' Coppery orange, medium sized, fragrant. Its ruffled petals give it great style. These, together with its wonderful colour, make it one of the most sought after roses of recent times.

'**Lincoln Cathedral**' Orange, pink, yellow, large, slightly fragrant. A new rose that has won national acclaim; may need some rain protection.

'**National Trust**' Crimson, medium-sized, little fragrance. A great bedding rose, lowish growing, strong stems, great for cutting.

'**Rose Gaujard**' Deep red, silver reverse, large, slightly fragrant. A tall and strong grower, and an ideal choice for bedding.

'**Silver Jubilee**' Peachy, pink, salmon and cream, with a large, fragrant rose that is the best of the recent varieties. Superb for bedding.

'**Solitaire**' Yellow with a touch of red on the tips, large, fragrant. Vigorous grower, almost rainproof, superb blooms for cutting.

'**Troika**' Orange-bronze, shaded red, large, fragrant. Very healthy, excellent bedding and cutting rose with good disease and rain resistance.

FLORIBUNDAS

'**Amber Queen**' Saffron yellow, fragrant. Low growing. Although new is a worldwide favourite. Healthy, dark foliage.

'**Ainsley Dickson**' Salmon pink with tones of red, slightly fragrant. Winner of the top prize of the Royal National Rose Society. Ideal for cutting and bedding.

'**Anne Cocker**' Vermillion, little fragrance. A good variety for bedding and cutting. Late flowering.

'**English Miss**' Silvery pink, very fragrant. Healthy with a flower in the style of a camellia. Free flowering with good repeat performance.

'**Escapade**' Soft rosy violet with white eye; fragrant. Unique and a great producer of blooms. Perfect as an individual bush or in a bed of its own.

'**Fragrant Delight**' Coppery salmon, very fragrant. Vigorous and upright with flowers that are almost hybrid tea shape. Very good bedding rose.

'**Iceberg**' White, medium size and slightly fragrant. One of the great roses in growth and flower production. Watch for black spot.

'**Korresia**' Yellow, fragrant, probably the best of all the yellow bedding roses with trusses of blooms that do not fade.

'**Margaret Merril**' Pearly white and very fragrant. High centered flowers, produced in plenty but they can develop spots in the rain.

'**Matangi**' Vermillion, white-eye, reverse of petals silver. Well-shaped buds and a very vigorous bush that can be kept lowish, but it will also grow tall if left with light pruning.

'**Memento**' Salmon vermillion, slightly fragrant. If you want a bright bedding rose this is it – compact with a great record of flower production.

'**Queen Elizabeth**' Pink, large blooms and slightly fragrant. One of the world's great roses – tall, stately and needing heavy pruning to be kept to a reasonable size.

'**Sexy Rexy**' Rose pink, slightly fragrant. Wonderful plant for bedding and cutting. Bushy grower and fine flower production.

'Southampton' Apricot-orange, slightly fragrant. Very vigorous and upright. A wonderful flower for cutting.

'Trumpeter' Orange red, slightly fragrant, probably the best of the red bedding roses, producing flowers right into winter. Great disease resistance.

MINIATURE ROSES

'Angela Rippon' Coral pink, bushy, healthy and a great flower producer.

'Baby Darling' Orange and pink blend and very popular.

'Baby Masquerade' Changes colour from yellow to pink to red. Very good.

'Darling Flame' Orange vermillion with golden reverse. Healthy, bushy.

'Rise 'n' Shine' Lovely yellow, lots of flowers. Also known as 'Golden Sunblaze'.

'Red Ace' Deep red and bushy grower that gives lots of flowers.

'Starina' Bright vermillion, the star of the miniatures.

Note: Other low-growing roses are often catalogued as patio roses, but they are very good in all parts of the garden. They are also quite new but contain some wonderful roses such as 'Sweet Dream' (peach-apricot rosette type), 'Sweet Magic' (orange with golden tints), 'Wee Jock' (deep crimson), 'Little Woman' (rose pink), 'Rosabell' (rose pink, quartered blooms), 'Gentle Touch' (light pink), 'Red Rascal' (scarlet-crimson) and 'Rugul' (yellow).

This list will go out of date as more and more of the American bred roses arrive on the market. Not included are the many little plants that are sold over the counter in numerous stores today. All can easily be increased by cuttings.

SHRUB ROSES

There is such a wide range of shrub roses in many different forms that it is impossible to give anything approaching a full range. The list that follows is therefore built round the roses recommended to the members of the Royal National Rose Society in its annual review, with the addition of a few personal favourites. They are all repeat flowering, unless specified.

'Aloha' Rosy salmon pink, slightly fragrant. Often named as a climber but does better when controlled by pruning and grown as a shrub.

'Anna Zinkeisen' Creamy white, fragrant. Vigorous shrub, growing to 1.2 m (4 ft) and a constant producer of lovely open flowers.

'Ballerina' Pink, white eye, little fragrance. Full heads of tiny white and pink flowers. Wonderful garden or tub variety. Perfect for mixed borders.

'Buff Beauty' Apricot to yellow, fragrant. Marvellous flowers in quantity. Perfect for single or group planting or in a mixed border.

'Canary Bird' Yellow, slightly fragrant. Arching stems of beauty. Needs plenty of room since it can grow to a large size.

'Cardinal Hume' Purple, slightly fragrant. Very unusual modern shrub that is good for hedging, in a group, or as a specimen bush.

'Chinatown' Yellow, touched pink, fragrant. Healthy, and disease and rain resistant. Bushy and tallish – good for the back of a border.

'Eyeopener' Red with yellow centre, slightly fragrant. Praised for flower and

'Canary Bird' is a shrub rose with clear yellow flowers.

foliage pleasing to 'fastidious garden planners'.

'Felicia' Light pink, fragrant. Carries fine trusses of bloom on a handsome plant and can be planted in a group, as a hedge, or individually within a border.

'Fred Loads' Vermillion, fragrant. The five-petalled flowers are carried in great trusses on strong stems. The plant can grow very tall.

'Fountain' Bright red, fragrant. Reliable – disease and rain resistant – although the stems can be a little thin and may break in heavy rain or strong winds.

'Frühlingsgold' Creamy yellow, fragrant. Although it is only a summer blooming variety it is one of the great roses with arching branches of large flowers.

'Joseph's Coat' Yellow to pink to red, slightly fragrant, medium-sized flowers. This if often regarded as a climber, but pruned back makes a good shrub for individual planting or in a border group.

'Mary Rose' Deep pink, slightly fragrant. One of the new English Roses. Shrubby with spreading plants and pretty cupped, petal filled flowers.

'Sally Holmes' Creamy white, slightly fragrant. Huge shoots, often with massive trusses of bloom held well above the foliage. Best in a close group of three or as a hedge for full effect.

Note: The range of shrubs could also be complemented by others of proven ability such as 'Nevada' (flowers in June with some repeat flowers in late autumn), 'Marguerite Hilling' (a pink sport of 'Nevada' and identical in all but colour), 'Pearl Drift' (a low, wide plant), 'Penelope' (light pearly pink, noted for its free blooms), 'Rosarie de l'Hay' (wine red, fragrant, tough), and 'The Fairy' (pink, spreading, and a wonderful low-growing rose).

CLIMBERS AND RAMBLERS

No climbing sports of bush roses are mentioned here, but a number of them are worth considering (see climbers in earlier part of this chapter). All are repeat flowering, unless specified.

'Albertine' Pale pink, very fragrant. Great early summer flowering rambler.

'American Piller' Pink, white eye, little fragrance. Rambler. Needs lots of care.

'Breath of Life' Apricot to apricot pink, slightly fragrant. Full hybrid tea type flowers.

'Compassion' Salmon pink to apricot, fragrant. Strong and stiff growth with big hybrid tea type flowers.

'Danse du Feu' Orange scarlet, little fragrance. Vivid colour, medium-sized blooms and a generous grower.

'Nevada', a fine shrub rose with creamy white flowers.

'Frühlingsgold' is a superb shrub rose with arching branches.

The lovely flowers of 'Handel', one of the best climbing roses of all time.

'Dublin Bay' Rich blood red, little fragrance. Slow to establish growth and can be used as a shrub as well as a climber. Superb flowers.

'Golden Showers' Bright to light yellow, fragrant. Dependable with good flower production rate.

'Gloire de Dijon' Buff yellow, fragrant. Big flowers of Victorian shape. Watch for mildew.

'Handel' Cream, edged rosy pink, slightly fragrant. The number one climber for growth, disease and rain resistance, and flowers that look lovely and cut well. Not rampant.

'Kiftsgate' White, fragrant. Extensive rambler. Flowers mid summer. It can be grown up a tree as it will tackle any height; and when it does it is generally impossible to prune. Best in large gardens where there is plenty of room.

'Maigold' Yellow, fragrant. Blooms only once and very early, but still a great favourite.

'Mme Grégoire Staechelin' Rosy carmine, very fragrant. Early summer flowering but the most generous of roses. Vigorous.

'Morning Jewel' Bright pink, slightly fragrant. A real eye-catcher with glowing colour and a good health record. Highly recommended.

'New Dawn' Shell pink, fragrant. Lovely clusters of bloom all summer long with some repeat flowers. Easy to grow, even from cuttings.

'Pink Perpetue' Rose pink, slightly fragrant. Free flowering with a pretty cupped flower in good trusses. Watch for signs of rust under the leaves.

'Rosy Mantle' Deep pink, fragrant. Large flowers with glossy foliage. A vigorous climber.

'Veilchenblau' Violet, fading to slate grey, fragrant. The most unusual of all roses. A spectacular rose in mid summer.

'Zéphirine Drouhin' Carmine pink, very fragrant. Pretty. Also known as the thornless rose. Must be watched for disease (black spot and mildew).

FLOWERS FOR CUTTING

It always seems an anomaly to talk about flowers for cutting. Shouldn't all flowers be for cutting? True, but many are better than others. Nasturtiums, for instance, make a wonderful display in the garden but they do not make good cut flowers; dahlias do. So too do sweet peas, chrysanthemums and dozens of others that can take you in an alphabetical list from *Achillea* to *Zauschneria californicia*.

In this chapter we look at the best methods of cultivation and some of the special types of flowers that make the finest decoration. There will be many more plants that you can use from annuals to bulbs, and most will be successful, but this is a list of the tried and trusted types of flowers, from the popular spring-time narcissus, to the end of the year chrysanthemums.

When it comes to cutting flowers it must be remembered that the sooner flowers are put into water the better they will be. The best time to take blooms is early morning or late evening. Give them some hours in deep water and then set about arranging them quickly but with care. With the thicker type of flower stem it is always effective to cut it under water, and to cut at an angle so that the stems will not sit on the bottom of the vase and so fail to take up water. If flowers begin to wilt they can often be brought back to life by placing them in warm water for a few minutes or, if the stems are woody, like roses, by holding them in boiling water for about a minute.

Here are the details of some of the more popular flowers for cutting. This is followed by a general list of some of the more unusual types that are worth trying, and with the appropriate methods of cultivation.

'Tête à Tête', a variety of *Narcissus cyclamineus*

MAKING A SELECTION

Narcissus

The flower that everyone knows, everyone can grow, everyone cuts, and is the herald of spring (it is actually called a daffodil when the centre trumpet is as long or longer than the petals). There is an exciting range of types now available in colours from pure white to delicate pink, and in blends of these colours. They grow from a few centimetres up to 60 cm (2 ft).

Choose a well-drained and sunny position to get the best from them. Plant from August to September, the earlier the better. Give them a generous hole (recommended depth is three times the size of the bulbs) in a well-cultivated piece of land. Generally they can be left undisturbed for a number of years, but when the clumps get too big and provide more foliage than flowers they should be lifted and divided. Many growers do this each year when the leaves have died down. Remove the smaller bulbs from the parent – if they are placed in an out of the way part of the garden or a nursery bed they will grow to flowering size in a year or two. Bulbs can be given some soluble fertilizer when the flowers have died down, which will build them up for the following year. The foliage should only be cut away when it has died down completely. In a dry summer the ground where the bulbs are resting should be watered deeply.

Red tulips underplanted with wallflowers make a cheering display in spring.

Narcissi are ideal companions among rhododendrons, their colouring contrasting well with the pink, red and purple flowers of the bushes. Look and see the wide range available each autumn; as well as the old favourites the gardener will find a wealth of new types that deserve a chance. However, the newer varieties can be quite costly.

Here is a selection to choose from.

Trumpet narcissi (daffodils) 'King Alfred' (yellow), 'Beersheba' (white) and 'Newcastle' (bicolour).

Large-cupped narcissi 'Carlton' (yellow), 'Silver Lining' (white), 'Fortune' (bicolour).

Small-cupped narcissi 'Frigid' (white), 'Mahmoud' (bicolour) and 'La Rianta' (bicolour).

Double narcissi These have more than one ring of petals, which are identical to the cup – 'Golden Ducat' (yellow), 'Snowball' (white), 'Texas' (bicolour).

Triandrus narcissi There are usually several flowers per stem. 'Liberty' (yellow), 'Thalia' (white) and 'Dawn' (bicolour)

Cyclamineus narcissi These can include many of the low-growing varieties. 'Peeping Tom' (yellow), 'Tête-à-Tête' (bicolour).

Jonquilla narcissi These have several flowers per stem, often known as jonquils, which are fragrant. 'Sweetness' (yellow), 'Golden Sceptre' (deep yellow), 'Bobbysoxer' (bicolour).

Poeticus narcissi Later flowering and very fragrant. 'Actaea' (yellow cup), 'Pheasant's Eye' (red cup).

Tulip
Like the narcissi the tulip is a fairly undemanding bulb that provides lovely flowers for cutting. It is planted slightly later (November or December) at a depth of about 15 cm (6 in), and in good soil. However, unlike narcissi, most tulip bulbs will improve with being lifted every year although some will continue to increase and bloom for a number of years if left alone. They should be lifted when the foliage has turned yellow. Store the dry bulbs in a frost-free place.

Every year there are new choices. Tulips are divided into a number of different groups, namely single early, double early, Triumph, Darwin, Lily-flowered, Rembrandt and Parrot, to mention just a few, all of which have their own cultivars within the groups. Probably the most popular are the Cottage Tulips, those old-fashioned tulips with the egg-shaped blooms that eventually open to about 13 cm (5 in) wide, and which come into flower from early May onwards. Although they are often as tall as 90 cm (3 ft) they have stout, strong stems that withstand all but the stormiest conditions. There is a wide

Left: *Tulipa greigii* has attractive foliage as well as shapely blooms.

Opposite: Dahlias are most effective when planted in a bed on their own.

range of colours available, from the strong red of 'Halcro', to the subtle light green, pink and purple softness of 'Artist'.

When mixed with forget-me-nots (*Mysotis*) and wallflowers (*Cheiranthus*) they can make a wonderful display in an island bed or border. There are so many combinations that work well with these flowers that the garden planner should never be at a loss, possibly turning to grape hyacinths (*Muscari*), white pansies (*Viola × wittrockiana*), or any of the grey-blue leafed plants such as catmint (*Nepeta*) or lavender.

The following list is compiled from popular kinds that are well proven.

T. clusiana (lady tulip) One of the many beautiful species tulips – and probably the loveliest of all with its greyish, grass-like foliage and the slender flowers that are white, flushed or streaked, with pink. There are some within the group that have more brilliant colouring than the parent species.

T. greigii A dwarf species with long-lasting flowers that are often mottled or streaked with purple-brown. Good for rock gardens and raised beds.

T. kaufmanniana Dwarf; blooms in March with a star-like flower. Ideal for the rockery. Bulbs do not need lifting in the winter.

T. fosteriana This species is known for its huge blooms which can reach 25 cm (10 in) when fully open. Species are creamy-white, but its hybrids are multi-coloured. 'Red Emperor', 'Easter Parade' (yellow), 'Stresa' (yellow with red band), 'Fritz Kreisler' (salmon pink) are the best known.

Darwin tulips Renowned for their brilliant colouring and strong stemmed robustness. 'Scarlett O'Hara' grows to 60 cm (2 ft) high; others to look for include 'Apeldoorn' (orange-red), 'Zwanenburg' (white), 'Jewel of Spring' (red, tipped yellow).

Lily flowered tulips Strong stemmed, weather resistant and very good for garden bedding. Long flowers have pointed petals that arch gracefully outwards. 'China Pink' (pink), 'West Point' (golden yellow), 'Arkadia' (buttercup yellow) and 'Queen of Sheba' (orange and red) are all to be recommended.

Rembrandt tulips So-called because they are flecked or streaked with another colour. They are often called Bizarre tulips, and with colours as in 'Victory' (yellow and brown) 'Gloire de Holland' (violet and white) or 'Absolon' (yellow and red) they can be quite a novelty in the garden.

Parrot tulips So-called because of their frilled petals. Unusual looking. Weak stem, many bicolours including 'Texas' (red, tipped yellow), 'Black Parrot' (blackish purple), and the pink and green 'Fantasy'.

Note: There are also many tulips that are sold as double-early, single-early, and double-late. There is a wide range to choose from, so with judicious selection the gardener can have tulips from early April until late May.

Dahlias
The dahlia is almost a specialist plant, taking such a hold on gardeners that they only want to raise these flowers, and nothing else. The first dahlia plants were sent from Mexico in the 18th century, and the generic name commemorates a Swedish botanist, Anders Dahl (1751–1787).

Over the years the dahlia has remained a constant favourite, adored for its late summer flowers, although different varieties have changed in popularity. Plant sizes vary enormously from about 30 cm (1 ft), to those that can reach almost 2.1 m (7 ft). The flowers too come in a wide range, from 2.5 cm (1 in), to a world-record size of over 53 cm (21 in).

Dahlia enthusiast go to great lengths to make sure that they have the perfect flower at the end of the summer, but for the ordinary gardener this isn't necessary. The plant requires very little help for a healthy display.

The plants can be grown from seeds, rooted cuttings or tubers. They should be started indoors in spring in gentle heat, being transplanted in late May or early June. They need a good soil which gets at least a few hours sunshine every day,

thorough watering and a liquid feed during the growing period. The taller dahlias will require staking, which should be done before planting. To increase the plant's bushiness, the growing tips should be pinched out when they are about three weeks old. If you want long stemmed plants nip away any side shoots two weeks later. Finally, disbudding (removing some of the flower buds) to produce fewer and larger flowers should be done when the flower buds are pea sized.

Dahlias should really be grown in a bed or border on their own to be truly effective, but they can also provide late colour in a mixed border at a time when the herbaceous flowers have mostly died down. Taller varieties are available for the back of the border, with smaller plants, such as Lilliput, useful for the front, which will bloom from late July until the first frosts.

DAHLIA CUTTINGS

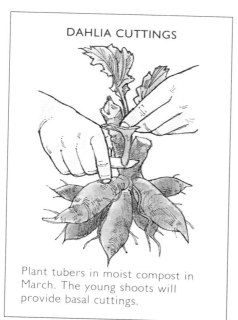

Plant tubers in moist compost in March. The young shoots will provide basal cuttings.

The flower heads are made up of miniature flowers, known as florets, and the type of floret is the key to identification.

There are many types of dahlias, from single-flowered, through collerette, to decorative and cactus. Here is a selection:

Single-flowered Made up of flowers of one ring of ray florets. Examples include 'Princess Marie Jose' (pink), 'Yellow Hammer' (yellow), 'Orangeade' (orange-red).

Collerette Very colourful, with an outer ring of flat ray florets, an inner ring of collar florets, and a central group of disc florets. Look out for 'La Giaconda' (scarlet and gold), 'Claire de Lune' (yellow and cream), and 'Chimborazo' (red and cream). For seed raising, try the Dandy strain, with its wide range of colours.

Decorative Full, double blooms on stems that grow between 90 cm (3 ft), and 1.5 m (5 ft). Try 'Jocondo' (purple, giant), 'Thames Valley' (yellow, large), 'Terpo' (red, medium), 'Gerrie Hoek' (pink, small), and 'David Howard' (orange, miniature).

Pompon Full, double, globe-shaped blooms, less than 5 cm (2 in) in size; the plant height is about 90 cm (3 ft). 'Hallmark' (lavender), 'Willo's Violet' (light purple), 'Noreen' (pink) are all good.

Cactus Full double blooms. Florets are narrow and pointing. Various sizes of blooms and plants. Consider 'Danny' (pink, giant), 'Irish Visit' (red, large), 'Appleblossom' (pale pink, medium), 'Doris Day' (red, small), 'Pirouette' (yellow, miniature).

Note: These are only a very small selection of the types of plant available. There are many varieties available to choose from. You could also contact the National Dahlia Society through the Royal Horticultural Society in London.

Dianthus

There are various forms of dianthus – sweet William (ideal as a cut flower and easy to grow as an annual or biennial), alpine pinks and annual carnations. The straightforward dianthus is well known to most gardeners as the old fashioned pink and few gardens would be without these or

Dianthus 'Doris' is one of the best of the modern pinks.

CUTTINGS OF PINKS OR BORDER CARNATIONS

Take cuttings or 'pipings' from side shoots in June. Strip foliage from the lower section of the cutting; make a suitable hole in sandy soil or compost with a dibber and firm in.

the modern pink. While they are better for garden flowering, many can still be well worth growing for cutting.

There are a few growing points that should be remembered. The plants do not do well with a damp mulch under them; they need full sun; and they only need water in exceptionally hot summers. Most of the plants lose their vigour after a few years, but nearly all can be grown on from non-flowering sideshoots in late summer. The flowering period is June to July in the warmer parts of the country.

The best of the modern pinks are 'Doris' (pale pink with salmon ring), 'Daphne' (pale pink, crimson eye), 'Cherry Ripe' (deep pink and double), 'Alice' (white, maroon eye), 'Haytor' (white), 'Robin' (scarlet), 'Valda Wyatt' (lavender double), 'Bovey Belle' (bright purple double). These are all quicker growing than the older pinks, and also provide good crops of autumn blooms.

Delphinium

The large flowered hybrids of modern delphiniums barely resemble their wild ancestors. The huge, tall spikes of stately beauty, with large flat flowers, often with a contrastingly coloured eye, have an ex-tended colour range that goes through all shades of blue and purple to yellow, pink and red. Today the delphinium waves its own magic power over the borders in every type of garden. They are quite stupendous when grown in groups in a mixed border, when grown side by side with all the usual border plants, and at the back of a border of roses they are truly eye-catching. Their association with roses goes so deep that the Royal National Rose Society has recently planted many varieties in their beautiful gardens at St Albans.

They may not be the easiest plants to grow, but the dramatic effect they achieve in both the garden and as cut flowers is worth the trouble. They need a well-drained, fertile and sunny site, preferably with some shelter from strong winds. However, even with shelter they will need staking when the plants are quite young.

Plant in the early spring, giving protection from slugs, otherwise the young plants will disappear almost overnight. The flowering period is June and July, but if the plants are cut back there will be another flush of blooms in the autumn. At the end of autumn cut the plants to ground level. As many will deteriorate with age, the solution is to lift the clumps in spring and divide them, replanting the most vigorous parts. They may also be raised from basal cuttings.

It is possible to raise plants from seed which will last for a few years. The 'King Arthur' (purple with white eye) and the Pacific Giants group are well worth growing. The Belladonna types are also easy to raise from seed – a packet will produce many different plants in various tones of blue. The difference between these and the large-flowered hybrids is that they are much smaller, and not as unwieldy, but they lack the magnificence of the bigger plants. The flowers carried in branching heads are cupped, rather than flat, in form. Look for the strains Pink Sensation and Blue Bees. The best plants obtained from the seed should be selected and planted in the border where they will last for some years.

The delphinium is another flower that is constantly being improved by breeders who import added attraction to its stately beauty. Among the most recent introductions is one in true delphinium blue, bred by an amateur member of the British Delphinium Society. It grows to 1 m (3 ft 6 in), and is named 'Clack's Choice'.

Delphiniums, the traditional blue-flowered herbaceous perennial for the border.

Plant selections vary from one catalogue to another, but these are some of the most impressive. A check should be made on their eventual height as some varieties grow from 2.4–3 m (8–10 ft), while others stay at hip to shoulder height. 'Skyline' (sky blue with white and blue eye), 'Vespers' (blue mauve), 'Butterball (cream), 'Blue Tit' (blue), 'Galahad' (white), 'Black Knight' (rich purple with darker eye), 'Clifford Lass' (pink), and 'Gemma' (lavender and mid-blue).

Sweet pea

Probably the most prolific plants for producing flowers for home decoration (and for your local show) are sweet peas (officially named *Lathyrus*). One spike alone can produce a bowl full of blooms. Plants can be raised from seed in a number of ways, either in a cold greenhouse from October onwards, in a garden frame or cloche from February to April, or outdoors in the flowering position from March to April.

Sweet peas have hard seeds, so to improve the rate of germination they benefit from being soaked in water overnight; if you find they are still very hard, they can be chipped with a sharp knife. Sow the seeds about 13 mm ($\frac{1}{2}$ in) deep in a humus rich soil in a sunny position, and keep them watered, particularly in dry weather. This is another case of the deeper prepared ground, that incorporates plenty of manure or compost, producing better flowers. The plants also require regular feeding – liquid feed applied every 10–12 days will prevent some of the troubles to which they can fall prey, such as bud fall. And finally, a good thick mulch of well-rotted manure or compost, applied in May, will conserve vital moisture for the plant, but do make sure that the mulch is kept away from the stems of the plant.

Young plants should be protected from slug damage, and be supported with twigs to encourage climbing. Approximately three to six weeks later the final, larger supports – 1.8 m (6 ft) high – should be put in place. They can be made of either canes or plastic netting. To achieve bushy plants nip out the top growth when the plants are about 10 cm (4 in) high.

You should take your cut flowers when the bottom bloom on each stem is in full colour. If the flowers are not cut they should be removed as soon as they fade to encourage new growth.

Your choice of sweet pea will be dictated by what the various seed companies offer. Those to look out for, by common consent, are the Spencer strain. A selection within this group include 'Air Warden' (orange-scarlet), 'Winston Churchill' (crimson), 'Leamington' (lavender), and 'White En-sign' (white). There are several dwarf varieties – look for 'Little Sweetheart', 'Snoopea', 'Peter Pan', and 'Bijou'. These are low growing and are mostly very fragrant. They also combine well with other annuals such as clarkia and candytuft, and the blue cornflowers.

Beginners should have few problems in growing good sweet peas; but if you can

Sweet peas provide an excellent source of flowers for cutting.

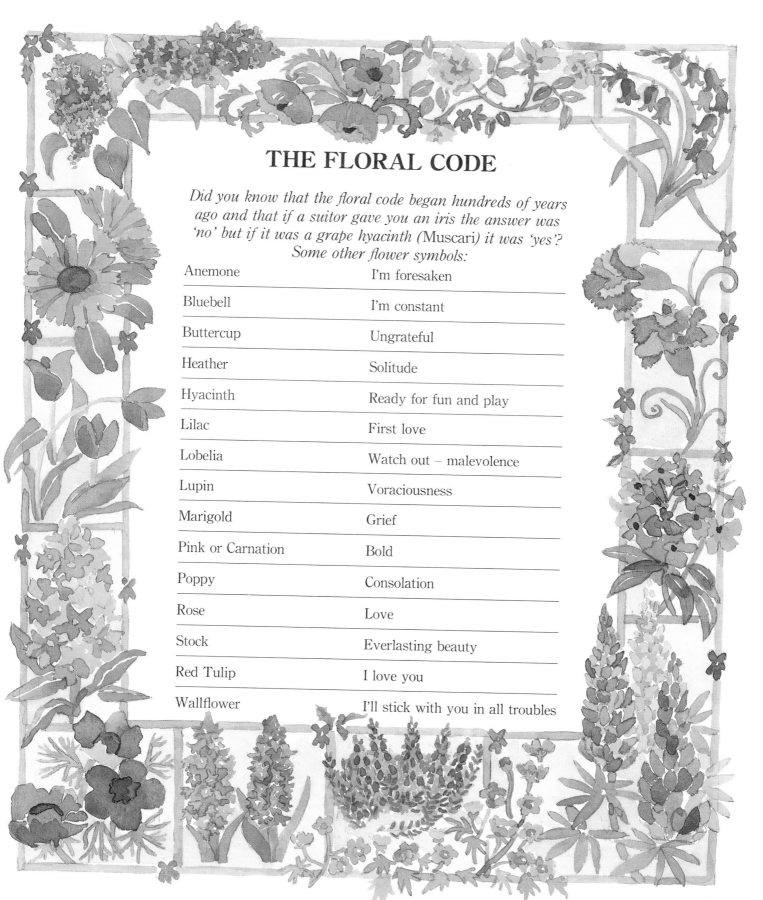

THE FLORAL CODE

Did you know that the floral code began hundreds of years ago and that if a suitor gave you an iris the answer was 'no' but if it was a grape hyacinth (Muscari) it was 'yes'? Some other flower symbols:

Anemone	I'm foresaken
Bluebell	I'm constant
Buttercup	Ungrateful
Heather	Solitude
Hyacinth	Ready for fun and play
Lilac	First love
Lobelia	Watch out – malevolence
Lupin	Voraciousness
Marigold	Grief
Pink or Carnation	Bold
Poppy	Consolation
Rose	Love
Stock	Everlasting beauty
Red Tulip	I love you
Wallflower	I'll stick with you in all troubles

discuss your techniques with an expert at a local flower show, you should get even better results the following year.

Chrysanthemum
After the rose, the chrysanthemum is the most popular flower grown in Great Britain today. It's come a long way from its starting base in China, round about the year 500 BC.

The great glory of these plants is that they can be grown anywhere, from a rock garden to a window-box, and from a general border to a greenhouse. They come in annual form, being easily grown from seeds sown in February – for example, the Charm and Cascade kinds – or as herbaceous perennials – the Shasta daisy *(C. maximum)*, *C. coccineum* (also known as *Pyrethrum roseum*), and the autumn flowering *C. rubellum*. Chrysanthemums also include many specialist perennials. This means that they can be grown outdoors from the summer, right through to October, and after that under cover. Within these groups they are sub-divided into many classes, sections and sub-sections. But for the real chrysanthemum lover, the growing season is from late summer to winter.

Chrysanthemums are easy to grow for the uninitiated. It is when enthusiasm rises above the ordinary garden level and the competitive edge takes over, that they

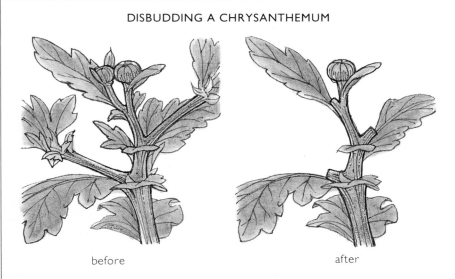

STOPPING A CHRYSANTHEMUM

When plants are about 20 cm (8 in) tall the soft growing tip should be pinched out. This will increase the number of flower-bearing side shoots.

really do become the ultimate challenge for the exhibitor. The flower gardener will be dealing mainly with the outdoor chrysanthemums which grow in the open ground without protection from summer until September.

These include those with small flowers which can sit at the front of a border, and those with decorative sprays of blooms for garden display which may need staking. Certainly, if decoratives are to be used for cut flowers, they will need staking, some pinching out of the top growth when the plant is about 20 cm (8 in) high, and disbudding, in order to produce one specimen bloom on a stem. It may seem like a lot of work to produce these superb flowers, but in fact is relatively easy and any half-enthusiastic flower gardener will be prepared to put in this amount of work for the ample rewards. If you have a greenhouse the rewards can be even greater, for there is a large group of chrysanthemums, called late-flowering, which normally bloom between October and late December, and which also provide a fine display.

When deciding where to grow your chrysanthemums aim for a well-drained but moisture retentive soil, in an area that receives some hours of sun each day. The plants prefer slightly acid conditions with plenty of organic matter dug into the top spit. Later, they may be propagated by dividing the roots or as rooted cuttings. When dividing a plant the outer portions of the stools can be taken away, and they will make satisfactory plants, although the rooted cutting method produces the better plant quicker. To take cuttings the stools should be overwintered in a cold frame or greenhouse. From new shoots at the base of the plant (not the sides) take cuttings

Disbudding chrysanthemums allows large, specimen blooms to develop.

DISBUDDING A CHRYSANTHEMUM

before

after

This is carried out to ensure the production of one superb bloom per stem. Leave the main bud untouched but take out each unwanted lateral shoot.

FLOWER TYPES OF CHRYSANTHEMUM

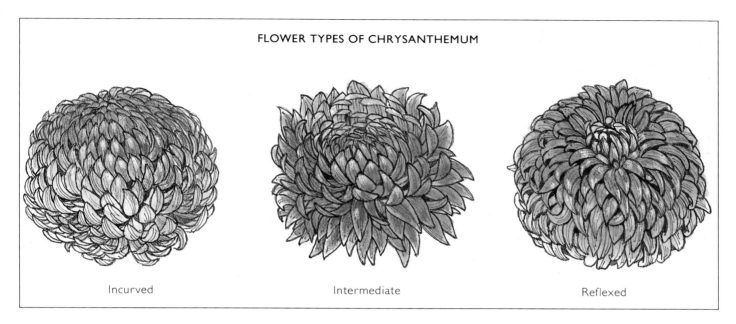

Incurved   Intermediate   Reflexed

which can be rooted in a heated propagator, and then transferred into pots where they should be regularly and thoroughly watered before being planted out in the border.

Watering in dry spells and feeding every 12 to 14 days with a soluble fertilizer is the way to bring the best out of the plants, which will also appreciate a mulch of peat or compost.

Slugs and birds can cause problems (see page 91), so act now before it is too late. The main trouble, however, is caused by the eelworm, which reveals itself in a blackening of the foliage. If it appears the plants *must* be destroyed to stop it spreading, and the ground should not be used for planting chrysanthemums again as this organism persists in the soil in a dormant form for many years.

Well-rooted cuttings of chrysanthemums can be purchased at a very reasonable price and provide an ideal way to get started. There are also numerous chrysanthemum societies throughout the country where the ordinary gardener is as welcome as the top exhibitors.

Because of the number of new cultivars being introduced each year and those being withdrawn there is a problem – as with most flowers – of giving a really up to date selection of plants.

In the meantime I will recommend one in particular – it is the decorative, incurved, large-flowered yellow called 'Derek Bircumshaw'. And in addition, here is a brief list of just a few of the likely winners for those who want to grow the decorative types.

Incurved
The florets are turned towards the centre, the blooms forming a tight ball.
Medium-flowered – 'Martin Riley' (yellow), 'Nancy Matthews' (white).
Large-flowered – 'Derek Bircumshaw', 'Evelyn Bush' (white).

Intermediate
This type of chrysanthemum has irregularly incurved and loosely held florets.
Medium-flowered – 'Cricket' (white), 'Claret Glow' (deep-pink).
Large-flowered – 'Keystone' (purple), 'Escort' (red).

Reflexed
The florets are turned outwards and downwards from the centre.
Medium-flowered – 'Karen Rowe' (pink), 'Regalia' (rosy-purple).
Large-flowered – 'Tracy Waller' (pink), 'Abundance' (yellow).

For those who just want a good outdoor display, the following will give fine results. 'Allbright' (bright yellow, spiky reflex), 'Bessie Rowe' (large incurving white), 'Promise' (rose purple incurve), 'Lilian Hoek' (bright-orange, bronze, decorative spray) and 'Orangeade' (golden orange reflex).

Other plants
As well as these very popular flowers there are numerous others that are superb for providing cut flowers. Many of these are annuals. (Look through pages 16 to 22 where you will find a rich collection.) Others include such wonderful flowers from corms, such as gladioli, and bearded and other kinds of iris, and perennials such as Russell Lupins.

Here is a brief outline of some of the needs and characteristics of these plants selected to keep your house full of flowers throughout the summer.

Asters (Michelmas daisy)
Pink and lavender coloured with a yellow centre, autumn flowering, and easy to grow is the usual description. But this isn't entirely true. Other colours are available, notably lavender-blue, red and mauve, for instance, and not all *Asters* are Michelmas daisies. Nor do they all grow in the late autumn – some of the *Asters* will bloom as early as July – *A.* × *frikartii* and *A. amellus* in particular.

A. novae-angliae and *A. novi-belgii* are the true Michaelmas daisies and can be difficult to grow being prone to disease, particularly wilt and powdery mildew (see page 92). However, you should not let this deter you from growing them. One of their advantages is that there are a number of different varieties that can grow from dwarf plants to giants that reach to 1.2m (4ft) high. Good sun and a

Left: Sedum and
Michaelmas daisies
– the opening of
their flowers
marks the end of
high summer.

Opposite:
Aster × frikartii,
rudbeckia and
sedum in full
flower.

Below: The star-
like bracts of
Astrantia major.

well-drained site are needed.

Propagate by dividing clumps in the autumn or spring.

Astrantia

Although this plant has its critics, the Astrantia major has still been a great garden favourite for hundreds of years. It is highly regarded as a cutting flower, with tall stems of 60–90 cm (2–3 ft) high flowers rising above clumps of coarse leaves consisting of three leaflets. The flowers are quite small, being a 2.5 cm (1 in) collection of tiny pink and white florets surrounded by green and white bracts or leaves that look like petals.

There are a number of different cultivars available, and they all grow well in ordinary garden soil that is kept free from slugs and provides dappled shade.

Propagate by division of clumps between late autumn and early spring. Seeds may also be sown under glass, but they will take at least 18 months to bring to flowering size.

Gaillardia

This is the fiery coloured daisy-like flower that can be seen in just about every border, where it lives up to its popular name of the blanket flower. Apart from the older *Gaillardia aristata* there are a number of dazzling cultivars in a variety of colour combinations. Flowers grow to about 60 cm (2 ft) high, and may need some staking as the weight of the flower can bend the stems. However, they are excellent for cutting.

To get them growing correctly they need a light, sandy soil and full sun. The stems must be cut to ground level when flowering has finished in September, and should be lifted and divided to avoid deterioration. They can be grown from seeds.

Gladiolus

Also known as the sword lily, this yields wonderful cut flowers. The one problem, however, is that the flowers have a short full-bloom life, and they are not quite right

for mixing in a border. It is therefore better to place them in a special bed where they can be staked and cared for as individuals. The best way to tackle the brief flowering problem is to stagger the planting of the corms from March to May, which should result in flowering from July to September. They need a well-drained site, rich soil, and plenty of sunshine, as well as some protection from strong winds. Corms should be lifted at the end of October, checked for any sign of disease, dried and housed in frost-free conditions.

There are five main groups, ranging from the large-flowered hybrids – which will grow anything up to 1.2 m (4 ft) high – to the miniatures – which can be as small as 30 cm (12 in). Within these groups there are scores of different varieties.

Gypsophila

This plant is often called baby's breath and is the background for many flower arrangements. Its tiny flowers on thin stems with greyish green leaves are the ideal acompaniment to most floral decorations. Generally accepted as the best of the varieties outside the species, *G. paniculata* is the double flowered and pure white 'Bristol Fairy'. It needs a gritty, limey soil deeply cultivated in a good sunny position to grow well. Once it has become established it will not transplant well and should be propagated by seed, basal cuttings in spring or stem cuttings taken and grown on in a cold frame in the summer.

Iris

The tall growers which are placed in the herbaceous border are grown from a rhizome, while the bulb types produce smaller varieties that can be planted at the front of a border. However, all are a delight to the flower arranger who is prepared to lavish attention on them, and who is not going to be too disappointed if some prove to be less than hardy.

The initial problem is one of too much choice – there is a different type of iris for just about every spot in the garden, so you must know which type you want. *Iris kaempferi*, for example, is a beautiful water-loving specimen that needs sun, warmth, and to grow in about 15 cm (6 in) of water. The valuable *I. pseudacoruus* (known widely as the yellow flag) also needs a moist spot – it is also commonly known as the *fleur-de-lys*, the emblem of the Kings of France and of the Boy Scout movement. *I. xiphioides* (the English iris), with shades of blue, violet and purple, and a central gold stripe, is excellent for group plantings, especially on account of its grey foliage. *I. xiphium* (Spanish iris) is more wide ranging in colour – blues, white, yellow, bronze and bicolored – and also looks good in single or mixed colours.

You can propagate the latter two irises by division, when the foliage has died down. *I. germanica*, the bearded iris, stately and interesting, will grow in just about any good soil, but if left in moist

Left: Tall growing bearded irises in a herbaceous border.

Opposite: An eye-catching combination of colours featuring Lilies and lady's mantle (*Alchemilla mollis*), with *Lysimachia punctata* in the background.

soggy land it can easily develop an infection.

Look out for the lovely frilled and ruffled 'Dancers' Veil' (blue and white) and 'Royal Torch' (violet with an unusual blue beard). You should also look for details of new varieties in the horticultural press; in the 1988 Royal Horticultural Society's Summer Show the sensation was a new golden yellow iris, with chocolate veining of excellent form, regarded as a great breakthrough. This has not been named at the time of writing, but it does show that there are new cultivars of most flowers that the inspired gardener ought to buy.

Lilium

Within this genus there is a wonderland of types that can provide a magnificent diversity in the garden, and exceptional cut flowers. Once regarded as hard to grow, the modern hybrid lilies have spread the gospel of wonderful colours and wide-ranging fragrances (don't expect that they will all smell delightful – some are obnoxious!), at heights from 30 cm (12 in) to 1.8 m (6 ft).

Since bulbs must never be allowed to dry out, plant them immediately after purchase. October is the best month for planting, when the soil is still frost free. Plant them about 15 cm (6 in) deep in well-cared for soil that gets sun and some shelter. You should then be rewarded with the exciting sight of, for instance, clumps of *Lilium candidum* (Madonna lily) with its pure white, fragrant flowers that carry a golden centre. Another excellent lily is *L. regale* (regal lily) with unrivalled clusters of wine red flowers which, when they open in July, show the pure white interior with a deep yellow throat and golden stamens. All the bulb requires is a sheltered site on good soil. You should also think about planting the giant Bellingham Hybrids that require a shaded, moist spot in the garden for their light orange, crimson spotted flowers.

Some of these wonderful flowers may be attacked by botrytis disease (this applies especially to the Madonna lily which will require regular spraying. The message for the summer is therefore to keep the lilies watered, and occasionally to add a liquid or soluble fertilizer). Divide mature clumps in the autumn and replant straight away, although you may not get flowers the following year. Note that you can also grow some lilies from seed.

Lupinus

This is the flower that everyone immediately associates with the cottage garden. Lupins are quick growing, tolerant of most conditions, and are available in a wide range of colours including pinks, blues, yellows and bicolours. The man who deservedly gets the credit for the great lupins of today is George Russell, who selected them from plants growing on his allotment in the 1930s, and who has given the world a range that bears his name.

Left: Russel lupins with the beauty bush (*Kolkwitzia amabilis*) – a perfect partnership for a pink border.

Opposite: Pink pyrethrum, more correctly called *Chrysanthemum coccineum*, growing with helenium in late summer.

Lupins grow with large, densely packed masses of bloom, and survive provided the slugs and mildew can be kept at bay. They prefer a slightly acid soil and can be grown from seed or from basal rooted cuttings. Generally the purchase is from a mixed selection of Russell Lupins, but single colours are also available.

The Woodfield Strain of new generation lupins are worth searching for, and are regarded as being the best of the modern selections for flowering from the bottom to the top of the spikes, and retaining their freshness over a long period. Since nearly all lupins reseed very easily, the seed heads should be taken off before this happens – the removal of the flower spikes will also lead to reflowering. Interestingly, as the result of a flood in a New Zealand nursery some years ago, Russell Lupins have been washed all over that country and are almost an environmental hazard!

Matthiola

Most gardeners will know this better as stock, that versatile and heavily scented flower that is now part of a wide range of plants that can be brought to flower from spring to autumn, and on through winter if you have a greenhouse. *Matthiola incana* is the general bedding type, while *M. bicornis* is night scented stock, but not nearly as interesting to look at as *M. incana*. These plants do not ask for much,

just a decent, not too acid soil in any bed, border or open garden. The only problem is getting them started! Seeds need to be watched and the instructions followed to the letter as some may be hardy annual, others half-hardy, and others biennial. Concentrate on those with double flowers, and handle the seedlings very carefully.

Pyrethrum

The flower arrangers' delight, now classified as *Chrysanthemum coccineum*, although the older name remains in popular use. It is also known as feverfew (as is *Matricaria*, a half-hardy annual which is also known as the mayweed and has a strange pungent smelling flower) because it was alleged to cure fever.

Pyrethrum has a long stem and good feathery foliage. Mainly pinks and reds, they like a lighter soil, well-drained and in full sun. They may need support, growing to about 90 cm (3 ft). The flowers should be cut as they fade. The prettiest are probably the singles – look for 'Bressingham Red' (crimson), 'E.M. Robinson' (pale pink), and 'Brenda' (deep pink).

Rudbeckia

You can have any coloured coneflower as long as it is in the yellow and orange range! The flower is also listed among the half-hardy annuals, which can be quite similar. The perennial has long-lasting, non-fading colour in August and September, and the flower, spiky petalled with a darker eye, is well clothed in foliage along the stem. They vary in height from about 60 cm (2 ft) upwards, and will grow without too much fuss in reasonable soil and in full sun or

The perennial rudbeckia makes a colourful addition to an autumn display.

dappled shade. Divide the clumps every three years in autumn or spring, and stake the flowers, especially the larger ones. Keep the flowers dead headed and cut the foliage back to the ground in September. The giant varieties include 'Golden Glow'; the more compact 'Goldquelle' suits the front of the border.

Scabiosa The flower that really echoes summer when used in floral decorations. The blooms are perfect for arranging and come in all shades of blue, darker mauves, as well as some white. The flowers have such a coolness, cleanness and delicacy about their frilly edged blooms that they have been called the 'pincushion of the garden'. They have also been known as the mourning bride, possibly because of the darker shades, and the roughness of the leaves which were supposed to cure itchiness. It is a perennial and is best planted in the spring about 45 cm (18 in) apart. It also prefers a limey soil and full sunshine, and may need some twiggy support in exposed places. The flowers should be cut for use in arrangements, but if they are allowed to fade on the plant they should be cut off to allow for new growth. The flowers will be produced from June to the first frosts. Propagate by division in the spring, or by basal cuttings. One of the most popular is 'Clive Greaves' – medium-blue, large flowered, long stemmed, growing to about 90 cm (3 ft). 'Miss Willmott' is a good white, while 'Moerheim Blue' and 'Imperial Purple' are also well worth considering. The only danger is from slugs.

THE ROCK GARDEN

Interest in growing rock plants has greatly increased in recent years. There are a number of reasons why this is so – in particular the introduction of new species and hybrids from their native habitats and the opening up of parts of China, Japan, other Asiatic countries and the Andes to botanists and the general public. It is now possible to obtain a wide selection of rock and alpine plants.

SITING A ROCK GARDEN

With the fast rising cost of land, large gardens get fewer and fewer, for the tendency is to build the largest possible number of houses in any given space.

Hence the attraction of rock plants, which, compared with most other plants, take up relatively little space. Even the smallest of gardens can be adapted to cultivate these small plants; the only drawback is where large, established trees are present. One often sees small mounds of soil planted with rock plants set among a few rocks placed almost up against tree trunks. No feature could be more doomed to failure, for in the matter of a year or so only the rocks will still be there – the plants will have disappeared.

Where possible, choose a site which is open and sunny and away from surface-rooting trees. The drip from these will rapidly cause a large number of plant

fatalities. If the garden is small or surface-rooting or surface-suckering trees are already established there – poplars, silver birch, elms or limes, for example – it may be necessary to grow the plants in troughs and other containers, raised above the ground and sited as far as possible from the trees. If the garden is in half shade (the kind of dappled sunlight to be found in a woodland clearing – full shade is not suitable), it is still possible to grow many of the low growing ericaceous plants, such as the dwarf rhododendrons.

A well-stocked rock garden in summer, showing how much colour and interest can be packed into a relatively small space.

Creating a small rock garden in a trough (or even an old sink) allows you to give the plants exactly the right growing medium needed for healthy cultivation.

DWARF RHODODENDRONS

There are many to choose from and the following are just a small selection. They will all tolerate light shade.

R. calostrotum
With its pink to purple flowers borne late in spring, it reaches 30 cm (1 ft) high.

R. 'Chikor'
A good dwarf hybrid with clusters of lemon-yellow flowers in late spring.

R. imperator
Very low growing, reaching only a few inches high and spreading to about 30 cm (1 ft). It has funnel shaped flowers in deep rose-purple which appear in late spring.

R. pemakoense
Possibly the dwarfest of all the rhododendrons. It has pinkish purple flowers.

R. radicans
Barely reaching 2.5 cm (1 in) in height, this carries large – for the size of the plant – single flowers, which vary in colour from light mauve to deep purple and show in late spring.

There is also a range of small hybrids available which are suitable for growing in this way.

For rhododendrons it is necessary for the garden soil to be lime-free, but here again such plants can be grown in troughs or other containers in a compost of four parts leafmould and one part lime-free loam and sand, these proportions to be by bulk, not weight.

RAISED BORDERS

In a small garden not large enough to accommodate a rock garden, it should be possible to build up border edges, especially if there is a small lawn. On a sloping site a small dry wall could be constructed, thus providing a two-level plot, which will enable a selection of trailing plants to be grown; for example, arabis, alyssum, the many colour forms of aubrieta, phlox, campanulas and helianthemums. These will give a wonderful display of colour starting in early spring and continuing through to summer. All these trailing plants can be underplanted with suitable dwarf bulbs, extending the flowering season over six months.

SOIL

Although it is seldom possible to choose the soil of one's garden, much can be done to make existing soil suitable for rock plants. The best medium is a light open soil with very free drainage. If possible, a lime-free soil is preferable, for lime can be added where this is required. Rock plants which approve of lime do not demand it, but lime-hating plants will only grow – and this is normally for a short period only – in specially prepared pockets of lime-free soil. So if you have an alkaline soil it is best to avoid growing all lime-hating plants. A rich loamy soil can be made ideal for the vast majority of rock plants by adding really coarse sand or small gravel, and, for really sharp drainage, a graded horticultural Perlite (an expanded volcanic rock that improves drainage and water availability, and aerates the soil).

If the soil is a heavy clay, it will be necessary to approach the problem in a different way. No attempt should be made to lighten it by adding drainage materials, a task which would perhaps be too difficult anyway. However, if there is a natural slope it can be turned to good use by digging a pit at the base between 20–25 cm

(8–10 in) deep and filling it up with some coarse rubble and then a layer of upturned turves or other such roughage to prevent soil washing down and blocking the drainage. The rock garden is then built up by about 20 cm (8 in) using a light, open compost. At least one quarter of the bulk of the compost around the drainage pit should consist of either leafmould or peat. This will provide an ideal spot for plants that prefer a greater quantity of moisture, such as Asiatic primulas.

Whatever soil is used over the clay it should have all perennial weeds removed; if this very important task is neglected, it will result in many back breaking hours being spent in attempting to remove them after planting has been completed, or, in bad cases, dismantling the rock garden with dire consequences to the plants. Nothing is more upsetting, for instance, than finding bindweed coming up in the centre of a dainty alpine plant.

CONSTRUCTING A ROCK GARDEN

It is difficult to give exact instructions on building a rock garden. A great deal depends on the available area and the type of rock employed. The actual construction must be left to the gardener's choice, and provided a few simple rules are followed the result should appear natural and aesthetically pleasing. Natural stone suitable for the rock garden is available in three types – limestone, sandstone and tufa. It makes sense to choose a source and type of rock which is reasonably near to hand, for rocks, expensive in themselves, are heavy and costly to transport.

First, the rock when positioned should have two exposed sides, one sunny, where plants can be placed which demand such a position to give of their best, the other in semi- or full shade for plants which require such conditions. Secondly, if the rock being used is limestone, which normally has distinctive strata, it should be placed almost horizontal to the surface, which gives it a natural look comparable to that of rocks in their natural surroundings. Lastly, do not overdo it, it is only necessary to have one or two outcrops in a small rock garden, which should be kept simple with the planting carried out round the highest point of the stone being used.

The next best rock to use (after limestone) is one of the local sandstones, which are found in many parts of the country; this is less costly and in many cases arrangements can be made to pick the stone up from the quarry, thus resulting in a considerable financial saving. Sandstone normally blends in better with the surroundings unless, of course, you live in a limestone area. If sandstone is used make sure that it is not composed of a large percentage of soft material, as this has a tendency to disintegrate after hard frosts.

Tufa is light to handle, extremely por-

Whatever rock you choose, remember that it must blend in well with its surroundings and should act as the perfect foil for the plants you wish to grow: this attractive ivy-leafed *Cyclamen hederifolium* stands out beautifully against the weathered rocks.

A cross section through a small rock garden showing the placement of the rocks and the way the plants have been positioned between them.

ous and easy to drill. A small chisel can also be used to make holes in it to take plants without causing too much root disturbance to those already planted. Place in the base of the hole a small amount of flaked leafmould and detritus removed from the piece of tufa when making the hole. When planting in tufa obtain small specimen plants, seedlings, or even rooted cuttings. Remove the plant from its container, taking care not to break too many roots, gently remove any loose soil, and insert the plant in the hole sideways, gently working the planting mixture around the roots and firming gently. Topdress with small pieces of tufa around the neck of the plant. This method of planting has been used successfully over many years, but tufa is costly. However, this is offset to a certain degree by its weight as it is much lighter than other mediums and easier to handle.

SCREE BEDS

Scree beds can be constructed as an edging to a lawn, flower border or path. With such features it is possible to grow a wide selection of dainty little plants without the use of a great deal of rockwork or even rocks at all. Wherever the beds are made they should be well clear of any trees, for the roots of the latter will quickly gain entry and exhaust the soil to the detriment of the rock plants. Scree borders should also be well away from the dense shade cast by buildings. Apart from these considerations, the actual aspect is not important, for there are many rock plants that can be cultivated in sun or semi-shade.

A scree bed is made by placing paving stones so that they form a box. Such a scree bed can be of any length to suit the site. The width should be at least 40 cm (16 in). The material to use in building up the 'shell' can be natural York stone, which is very expensive, broken paving stones or slabs of concrete. The paving stone should allow one to build a frame in which to grow a representative collection of rock plants. Once the size has been decided on, a base should be constructed to carry the walls. Depending on the width of the pieces of paving stone used, a layer of cement 6 cm (2¼ in) deep should be laid under these to form the base for the stones. This concrete base should extend about a further 8 cm

With a larger rock garden, it is a good idea to include a network of pathways in your design to allow access for planting, weeding and other maintenance.

A scree bed of colourful alpines makes an attractive edging for a gravel path in a sunny part of the garden.

(3 in) beyond the stones and be made smooth, thus forming a narrow path between the scree bed and the lawn. This will allow a lawn mower to be used right up to the wall of the scree bed.

When laying the base, holes for drainage must be made at regular intervals. To prevent pests such as slugs, woodlice and so on gaining entry, small pieces of perforated zinc should be placed over these holes.

Whatever stone is used, this should be fixed on the base by the use of a cement mix and the walls built to a minimum height of 20–24 cm (8–10 in). A few weeks after completion of the building the scree borders are prepared, as follows. First, a good layer of broken crocks or roughage is added, followed by a well-firmed layer of peat or leaf roughage to prevent the compost filtering down and blocking up the drainage. The border is then filled to the top with either of the following mixtures: for sun lovers and bulbs equal parts of loam, leaf-mould and sharp sand, and for plants that require half shade the same mixture with an equal quantity of peat added. In each case a small handful of bone meal is spread over the surface of the compost, well watered in and left to settle. After a week or so the scree border will be ready for planting.

Planting

The chosen plants, which must not be pot-bound, should be carefully removed from their pots, the drainage material in the base removed and a few roots teased loose. Remove some of the old surface compost, plant in a prepared hole in the scree border and make firm. The surface should then be covered with stone chippings. Finally, a few decorative pieces of rock will put a finishing touch to the border.

TROUGH GARDENS

Troughs are very popular today, but unfortunately the real thing is difficult to find and, if found, generally costly. However, any trough which is at least 12 cm (5 in) deep is suitable for growing a wide selection of rock plants. They can also be used to grow specimen plants or dwarf bulbs.

The compost required is similar to that used in the scree border, and the same

A peat garden is perfect for a collection of rhododendrons.

method is used in preparing the trough. Make sure that a lime-free loam or ericaceous compost is used if lime-hating plants are grown. Watering is very important, especially during the re-establishment of the plants.

THE PEAT GARDEN

A large number of plants requiring lime-free soil can be accommodated in this type of garden. The top 10 cm (4 in) of lime-free

A peat garden needs a layer of rubble for good drainage. Moist peat blocks form the walls.

soil in a semi-shaded part of the garden should be dug over, all roots removed and plenty of well-rotted leafmould or peat mixed in. Peat blocks are used to construct the wall, and blocks measuring 24 by 12 cm and 8 cm (10 by 5½ in and 3 in) deep are ideal. Make sure that they are moist. They should be laid as when building a brick wall and two layers are necessary. A compost of four parts leafmould or peat, one part fibrous, neutral loam and one part coarse sand is used like a cement mix, working it into all the cracks as the wall is being built. Fill the rest of the bed with the same mixture. After planting, topdress the bed with 3 cm (1¼ in) of moss peat and water the plants in. This bed should be kept moist at all times to give of it best.

A peat garden is an ideal place for primulas and rhododendrons. Some gentians like G. sino-ornata flourish there too.

DWARF SHRUBS

Mention should be made of the role of dwarf shrubs which can add shape, height and colour to the rock garden scree bed, trough garden or peat bed, and if evergreen kinds are mixed with deciduous ones this will provide interest during the winter months.

PROPAGATION

There are two main methods of increasing rock plants, by seed or cuttings.

Seed

John Innes seed compost is both a suitable and efficient germinating medium. A lime-free seed compost is also available. Seed of the normal types of rock plants is best sown in late February. This will provide the resulting plants with six months of growth during spring and summer so that they make sturdy specimens ready for planting out in early autumn. Seed should be sown thinly and covered with a fine dressing of sharp sand, and must be kept moist by immersing the seed pan in water, as necessary.

Cuttings

These also provide a ready means of increase, and in the great majority of cases green cuttings will root quite easily. They are best taken from small pieces of new growth, placed in a pot containing a mixture of equal parts sharp sand and fine peat. Where possible, they should be between 2–3 cm ($\frac{3}{4}$–$1\frac{1}{4}$ in) in length, the lower third of the stem being left clear of leaves (these leaves should be removed by giving each one a gentle upward pull). Insert the cuttings around the edge of the pot to a depth where the bottom leaves touch the rooting medium. Water the cuttings in well. Place a plastic bag over the whole pot and make firm with a rubber band. Rooting should take place in a few weeks, and signs of new growth will be evidence of this. The small plantlets are then grown on in John Innes No 1 potting compost or an equivalent until ready to plant in their permanent positions in the rock garden.

SELECTED PLANTS FOR THE ROCK GARDEN

The following selection should provide plenty of colour and interest. Look out for those that require a lime-free soil.

Aethionema 'Warley Rose'

This sub-shrubby perennial has fleshy leaves. The pinkish-red clusters of flowers arise in summer. An easy plant to grow. Propagate by seed or cuttings taken during summer. This is one for a chalky or limy soil – 15 cm (6 in).

Andromeda polifolia 'Nana'

This charming evergreen shrublet, with its narrow leathery leaves, silvery grey on the underside, is suited to both rock gardens and peat beds. Clusters of urn-shaped rose-pink flowers appear in May. It requires soil with a high humus content and can be increased by softwood cuttings planted in lime-free compost in summer – 5 cm ($2\frac{1}{2}$ in).

Arabis caucasica 'Rosa Bella'

A summer flowering perennial with grey-green, slightly toothed leaves. Best planted in a sunny position, 'Rosa Bella' has attractive reddish-purple flowers. Readily propagated by division or by cuttings taken during the summer – 15 cm (6 in).

Aster alpinus

A spreading herbaceous perennial plant with solitary flower heads, in summer, consisting of white or pink ray florets surrounded by yellow tubular disk florets. Grows well in limy soil. Propagate by division in spring or autumn – 15 cm (6 in).

Aubrieta

A graceful compact evergreen plant with grey-green foliage. The showy, semi-double flowers appear in spring. They come in shades of purple and mauve and make an attractive display. Faded blooms should be removed. Propagate by cuttings taken during spring or division in late summer – 10 cm (4 in).

Bellis perennis (double daisy)

This showy, neat, almost stemless herbaceous perennial plant has semi-double flowers in various shades of pink during the summer months. Young plants often flower better than old specimens and may be propagated by dividing the crowns after flowering – 10 cm (4 in).

Berberis × stenophylla 'Corallina Compacta'

A charming evergreen shrub suitable for the trough garden or rock garden. The attractive and abundant yellow flowers in spring are followed by purple fruit covered by blueish bloom. Propagation is by layering or by cuttings taken with a heel during summer – 15 cm (6 in).

Campanula (bellflower)

The massed display of flowers produced by C. carpatica is most attractive. Abundant, bright blue bell-shaped flowers ap-

The beautiful little gentian *Gentiana sino-ornata* is an excellent plant for the rock garden, provided you can give it lime-free soil.

pear over a long period during summer. Readily propagated by cuttings in spring or by division – 30 cm (12 in).

C. cochlearifolia is another summer-flowering perennial. This spreads by underground runners and sends up slender branched stems carrying the bell-shaped, blue flowers. The foliage is a fresh green. Can be increased by seed – 5 cm (2 in).

Cyclamen hederifolium
(C. neapolitanum)
The deep green leaves with silvery markings are most decorative; these persist well into the spring and appear after the dainty mauve flowers of autumn. A lovely cormous plant for naturalizing, which is usually long lived. New plants can be raised from seed – 10 cm (4 in).

Daphne cneorum (garland flower)
Tiny, trailing evergreen shrub with narrow deep green leaves, grey on the underside. The fragrant, rose-red flowers are borne profusely in spring. New plants can be raised by seed, or by cuttings of the previous year's wood taken in summer – 15 cm (6 in).

Dianthus
D. alpinus is a mat-forming pink which makes loose cushions of bright green, narrow, strap-shaped leaves. The large and attractive flowers show in summer. They vary in colour from white to deep pink with dark purple spots at the base of the petals. An attractive plant for the rock garden or trough increased by seed or by softwood cuttings taken during summer – 5 cm (2 in).

D. 'La Bourboule' is a delectable little tufted perennial plant with narrow silvery leaves which, together with the most attractive bright pink flowers in summer, make it a much admired plant for rock garden or container. Plants may be increased by cuttings taken during summer – 8 cm (3 in).

Erinus alpinus
This delightful tufted plant forms cushions of foliage with small pink flowers arising in spring. Ideal for crevices and the wall of a raised bed. Plants may be propagated by seed sown during spring. Plants may also be increased by division after flowering – 15 cm (6 in).

A mixed planting of yellow and purple varieties of *Iris pumila* – this tiny member of the iris family requires full sun if it is to thrive.

Gentiana (gentian)
G. verna is one of the most attractive of the many gentians available. The tufted perennial gives rise to delectable deep-blue solitary flowers in summer. Easily propagated by fresh seed sown in containers to remain out of doors during winter or by division – 10 cm (4 in).

G. sino-ornata is another beautiful little plant with prostrate stems ascending at the tips with deep blue, long funnel-shaped, terminal, solitary flowers in autumn. An excellent plant for ground cover on the rock garden and easily propagated by division or by sowing fresh seed. Needs an acid soil – 15 cm (6 in).

Geranium cinereum 'Ballerina'
This is one of the true hardy geraniums (not to be confused with the pelargoniums or bedding geraniums). An almost stemless herbaceous plant with attractively lobed leaves. The most attractive and abundant white flowers veined crimson arise in summer. Propagate by seed or by division in spring – 15 cm (6 in).

Geum × borisii
This herbaceous perennial forms a basal rosette of attractive leaves giving rise to bright orange flowers in summer. This is best increased by division in spring or autumn and is a lovely plant for the rock garden or raised bed – 30 cm (1 ft).

Helianthemum nummularium 'Wisley Primrose'
(rock rose or sun rose)

A spreading semi-shrubby evergreen much used to cascade over a dwarf wall and most attractive when planted at the edge of a raised bed. The attractive leaves are green on the upper surface and grey beneath covered with downy hairs. Abundant yellow flowers appear in summer. A useful plant which needs a sunny spot and should be trimmed back after flowering to avoid getting straggly. Propagate during summer by cuttings taken from non-flowering shoots – 30 cm (1 ft).

Iberis sempervirens (candytuft)
A bushy, evergreen sub-shrub with fragrant white flowers in winter. Plants can be raised by sowing seed, by cuttings taken in June or the rootstock can be divided – 60 cm (2 ft).

Iris pumila
The small rhizome gives rise to stout tufts of green, sword-like leaves. Miniature bearded-iris flowers appear in spring and summer and come in a range of colours from white to purple. Plant in full sun. Propagate by division of rhizomes after flowers fade in June – 5 cm (2 in).

Lamium maculatum (dead nettle)
A spreading evergreen perennial with underground stems giving rise to shoots with leaves attractively variegated in silver in the variety 'Beacon Silver'. The flowers are blue and carried in dense clusters. Readily increased by division or by striking softwood cuttings during summer – 38 cm (15 in).

Pulsatilla vulgaris, with its beautiful violet flowers, thrives in full sun and in alkaline soil, but does not like to be transplanted once it has been established.

Linaria alpina
An attractive, prostrate perennial with spurred, intense blue flowers with a deep yellow centre in summer and autumn. A most adaptable plant suitable for growing in a dry wall or rock garden. Propagate by division in spring, by seed or by softwood cuttings during mid-summer – 15 cm (6 in).

Lithospermum diffusum 'Heavenly Blue'
Evergreen sub-shrub with trailing stems which give rise to beautiful and abundant deep blue flowers in summer. Cut back when flowers fade to avoid a straggly appearance. It needs a lime-free soil. Propagate by cuttings taken from previous year's growth – 20 cm (8 in).

Lysimachia nummularia
A creeping evergreen perennial with trailing stems bearing roundish leaves. The bright yellow flowers appear in summer, being ideal as ground cover in the rock garden. It is also suitable for growing in a hanging basket or container. 'Aurea' has yellow stems and foliage. Divide in autumn or spring – 10 cm (4 in).

Oxalis adenophylla
A roundish bulb-like base gives rise to abundant greyish or silvery-green leaflets on long thin stems. Large, solitary, pink, bell-shaped flowers open in summer. An interesting and adaptable plant for a trough or scree garden in a protected position. Increase from offsets from the bulb-like base – 15 cm (6 in).

Papaver alpinum (alpine poppy)
A charming perennial with lobed leaves. The attractive white or yellow flowers appear in summer. Propagate by division in spring – 15 cm (6 in).

Primula
P. × juliae 'Wanda' is a charming early-flowering primula with bright purple-red flowers in spring standing clear of the dense mat of coarsely toothed, cordate leaves. Propagate by sowing fresh seed, the subsequent seedlings being potted firmly in well-drained compost which should be kept moist when growth is active. Remove dead leaves – 10 cm (4 in).

P. denticulata is another favourite primula whose sharply toothed, mealy-covered leaves grow to 30 cm (1 ft) long provided the soil is not too dry. Rounded heads of flowers come in various colours including white and shades of mauve, with yellow centres. Self-sown seedlings should be weeded out to retain the choicest flowers and the best selections can be increased by division – 20 cm (8 in).

Pulsatilla vulgaris (Pasque flower)
An almost black, fibrous rootstock gives rise to most attractive pinnate foliage. Beautiful violet flowers with yellow stamens terminate the long hairy stems. Fresh seed germinates readily and plants can also be increased by root cuttings taken in July – 15 cm (6 in).

Saponaria (soapwort)
A herbaceous perennial for the rock gar-den readily increased by cuttings with a heel in July. This choice little plant is slow growing and produces abundant pink flowers in summer. Best in a sunny position – 5 cm (2 in).

Saxifraga burseriana
A much admired little cushion-forming perennial. The dainty reddish stems arise through silver-grey leaves to produce reddish flower buds which open to display glistening white or pinkish petals in spring. Readily propagated by division and easily grown on in a raised bed or rock garden – 5 cm (2 in).

Sedum spathulifolium 'Capablanca'
Evergreen plant forming a dense cushion-like clump producing runners from the base. Leaves form a silver-white rosette, those on the erect flower stem are scattered, club shaped and spreading. Yellow flowers in summer provide a bonus to the attractive leaves. Propagate by division – 13 cm (5 in).

Sempervivum (houseleek)
A rosette-forming perennial up to 5 cm (2 in) across and composed of densely packed fleshy leaves with reddish or green tips. In the case of *S. arachnoideum* these are connected with cobweb-like hairs. Bright red flowers terminate an erect stem in summer. An easy plant to grow and multiply by division – 5 cm (2 in).

Thymus citriodorus (lemon thyme)
A lemon-scented evergreen shrub with attractive pale lilac flowers in summer. Plant in full sun and propagate by cuttings during late summer – 30 cm (1 ft).

Veronica spicata 'Incana'
This evergreen perennial is one of many useful plants within the genus. The leaves are toothed and the blue flowers appear in summer. Best in full sun. Increase by cuttings in summer – 20 cm (8 in).

Viola cornuta
The creeping stems give rise to large flowers with a slender spur. 'Alba' has white flowers. A prolific flowering plant and easily propagated by division or by seed – 30 cm (1 ft).

PESTS AND DISEASES

Troubles? Diseases? Pests? No matter what you call them, fortunately there is a remedy for all complaints. All you have to do is accurately identify the problem, and act promptly.

However, before we turn to specific problems, note that many are caused by ignorance of plants' needs. Remember frost is a problem to tender plants, and that an abundance or lack of water, too much sun or no sun, and poor feeding must be generally thought about. To thrive, plants must be healthy. If they are not healthy, they will not withstand the problems that are bound to afflict them at some point in their lives. But there are two main reasons for a lot of troubles, and these can't be stressed often enough, waterlogged ground and lack of hygiene. If the gardener can tackle these early on then many of the problems mentioned in this chapter will fail to materialize.

Here is a 10–point trouble-shooter's guide that will put you on the right path.

1. Buy the best plants available and make sure you know their likes and dislikes.
2. Before you think of planting, clean-up the garden. Get rid of weeds, old plants that will never be any good, and rubbish that may harbour pests.
3. Prepare the ground thoroughly. You will notice that the majority of plants named in this book need a well-drained soil. Never forget that.
4. Make sure that the soil and the planting time is right for your new plants. Most summer flowers should wait until the likelihood of hard frost is over. Water the soil first so that the plant is going to get immediate help to grow on. A plant that wilts is in trouble straight away.
5. Too many gardens show signs of plant starvation. Keep them regularly fed. A small amount of regular liquid feeding will do the plants a power of good. Applications of general fertilizer in powder or granular form should be done very carefully as it can scorch if it falls on the foliage. An absence of fertilizer results in bad plants, poor flowers and general disabilities. On the other hand too much feeding can result in too much foliage, and few flowers. Find the happy medium.
6. Foliar feeding is the way to help a plant immediately, overcoming a pest or disease attack. Spray on the leaves during a dry evening, never in full sun.
7. The man who wrote that you are nearer to God in your garden was very accurate – but you will be closer still if you are on your knees! Yes, by getting close to your plants you will soon spot the defects, the first pests, and the first signs that something is going wrong.
8. You do not always have to use chemi-

Keep your plants healthy and your garden full of flowers by following the trouble-shooter's guide (above).

Inspect chrysanthemums regularly as they may be troubled by several pests and diseases.

cals to overcome problems. Caterpillars can be picked off by hand. Keep an eye open for all ugly bugs! And if a plant dies in the garden immediately lift it and look for the reason – were the roots eaten away, does it look dry, are there bugs on it, or on the roots? Close inspection will provide the answer.

9. Slugs can be one of the worst marauders in the garden. They eat away young plants almost overnight, and once the foliage has been attacked there is no remedy. Put down chemical bait, or consult a local gardener to see how he or she tackles the problem.

10. Spray with care. Chemicals can be dangerous to you, your family, your neighbours, your pets and your plants. Never spray on a windy day, for even the slightest breeze will carry the chemical to nearby plants. A weedkiller can easily destroy other plants.

You should wear eye protection, even sunglasses are better than nothing, and gloves. Check that the chemical is right for your plants – some used on roses can kill fuchsias. Also, keep the spray off blooms if you can possibly manage it. Never store any chemical in a bottle or other container. And finally, make sure they are well out of the way of children who are naturally inquisitive.

Let us now look individually at some of the more likely trouble spots. I will not give details of the possible sprays you should use, but any reasonable plant store or garden centre will have a good range to choose from.

FOLIAGE TROUBLE MAKERS

Aphids

Don't just call them greenfly – they come in multicoloured hordes of green, white, black, pink, and yellow flies, and they sap the life from a plant. Spray thoroughly. There are two main insecticides – **contact** (which will kill off the living aphids but not the eggs that will hatch the next brood), and **systemic** (which gets into the plant so the next aphid that sucks the plant will pay the penalty). Don't believe the soapy water theory. It washes them off, but then they shake themselves dry and climb back on board again. They will ruin plants if not killed.

Caterpillars

They attack with a lack of discrimination. You can identify them by the irregular and often large holes eaten in the foliage. They are an early season invader. Pick them off if you can, but if not use a spray.

Earwigs

They are the curse to dahlias, chrysanthemums and roses in particular. They hide in the plants by day when you may be able to shake them out. If you put little bundles of straw on top of canes among the flowers they will nest there, so making it easy to dispose of them. Spray or dust to keep them at bay between May and October.

Make an earwig trap by filling a pot with straw and putting it on a stick among the flowers.

Slugs and snails

The major contenders as the real nasties. They too leave irregular holes in plant leaves and can also be spotted by their trails of slime, particulary over shady, poorly drained land. Avoid leaving them any hiding places in decaying rubbish. There are slug traps for anyone who doesn't want to lay down chemicals in the form of pellets or liquid slug bait. The slugs will fall in and drown in a saucer of beer. But clean and well-cultivated land is the best deterrent.

Capsid bugs

These attack many plants, such as dahlias and chrysanthemums. Tattered holes appear in the bottom leaves, and the foliage becomes spotted, puckered and distorted. Again, the message is be hygienic – rubbish and weeds will give the bug a hiding place, so clear all these away or burn them. Spray with a suitable chemical when the first signs are spotted.

Woodlice

These are to be found just about everywhere, and are night eaters that hide by day. Again, hygiene is the main method of prevention, although there are some very effective powders for eliminating the nests that expand quickly and easily in damp rubbish, or under wood or pots.

ROOT TROUBLES

These are unfortunately not seen until it is almost too late. But when any plant dies a check should be carried out on the soil for any of these bugs.

Vine weevil

Probably the 'new' curse for the gardener. It has long existed, but in recent years has increased enormously, attacking plant roots through their grubs. The adult is black, nasty looking and slow moving, and lives on the foliage, eating small irregular notches into the leaves during the night. The young turn into the nastiest attackers – wrinkled, creamy coloured, brown-headed grubs that exist in good peaty type soil. A plant will suddenly die and when examined will be found to have no roots. Search the soil and destroy.

The worst affected plants are primula, fuchsia, rock plants, pot plants of all sorts, and just about any plant with a tender root. There are various sprays and powders available for tackling this disaster, but the best way is to hunt them down and destroy. Also, clean up any hiding places and spray any wild ivy growing on walls and such like, where they are likely to be hiding.

Chafer grubs

These are similar to the vine weevil, but bigger. Curved, creamy, brown-head, with a silver tail, they live on the roots of herbaceous plants as well as dahlias and chrysanthemums. Sprinkle chemicals on the ground.

Millepedes

Black, brown and spotted, they tend to curl up when disturbed. They cause root damage but can be stopped in their tracks by one of the special slug-type chemicals that are also recommended for this root predator.

Leatherjackets

Pests that cause most trouble on heavy, wet soil, and early in a spring that follows a wet winter. Troublesome among the herbaceous plants. Treat as for millepede.

Cutworms

When a plant dies because the stem has been nibbled away this is the culprit. Once the problem is spotted look for a 5 cm (2 in) brown, greenish or grey sluggish insect and destroy.

ROOT DISEASES

Black root rot

This probably is most prevalent in the flower garden. It can be found attacking sweet pea, begonias, geraniums and others. The leaves turn yellow and the root will die and turn black. It most often occurs where the same type of plants have been repeatedly grown in the same area. Rotate plantings to avoid attack.

Club root

A serious disease that can affect flowers, although it will be mainly found in the vegetable garden. The roots become swollen and plants will be undersized and die when young. Improve the drainage, adding lime for possible control, but it might be necessary to sterilize the soil.

Other root diseases

There are some other root diseases that are specific to particular plants and areas, but the above mentioned are the commonest. Of course root troubles often begin above ground too, and a plant attacked by a fungus or disease such as rust will eventually stop growing, and the root growth will therefore be affected.

Storage rots

Various rots can set in through bad storage (this allows fungal attacks), or through the bulbs being grown on in waterlogged conditions. Daffodil bulbs can be affected with the narcissus fly – if bulbs are soft when lifted or show distress when growing, they are probably being attacked by the maggot of this fly. Control is not easy, but soft bulbs should be destroyed and the ground cleaned up around the dying foliage. Any soft bulbs, corms, tubers, or rhizomes should be destroyed.

Tubers of the dahlia can be affected by fungal rot. To prevent this stand the tubers upside down when lifted, and allow them to dry out thoroughly. There are sprays that can be used, and again the tubers must be left to dry before being stored. Any badly diseased parts can be cut away and destroyed.

STEM AND LEAF TROUBLES

Many will be caused by some of the pests already mentioned, the aphids being the main source of the problem. However, other troubles will be caused by diseases such as mildew and rust that must be controlled immediately. The commonest disease is mildew, with either powdery or downy symptoms.

Powdery mildew

This can be seen in gardens where there has been a lot of rain, and even in gardens where the roots have been allowed to dry out. It appears like a white mould on the leaves, eventually distorting the foliage.

The great thing is that it can be easily controlled by a number of very good systemic sprays. The initial spraying should be followed up by another within 10 days, and if the instructions with the product are followed the damage can be minimized. Roses, delphiniums and daisies all fall prey to the powdery mildew.

Powdery mildew on a rose.

Downy mildew

In damp weather some flowers are also likely to fall prey to downy mildew. Yellowing patches on the leaves, followed by a greyish growth of mould under the leaf, will give the warning, and unless tackled immediately plants can be ruined. A different spray is needed here, so specify your problems before purchasing any chemical treatment.

Rust

A real killer, especially of roses, but also geraniums, carnations, chrysanthemums. It often appears in just one section of a garden, and will not spread, even to similar varieties of the affected plant. It is easy to identify, for it creates foliage spots which are a bright, rusty colour. If allowed to develop the rust spots gather until they have covered the surface, and then become black and fall off like rust from metal. Spraying must be repeated regularly.

Botrytis

This is a grey mould that destroys plants by attacking foliage and stems. Remove the leaves, and if a stem is affected cut below the mould and destroy the mouldy material. Systemic fungicides are the only answer.

Stem rots

There are other types of stem rot in which parts of the stem decays. This is most common in herbaceous plants. It can be recognized by black raisin-like growths inside the stem. The only solution is to lift the plants and destroy them.

Foot rot

This will be spotted by the blackening of the stem base, and from then on it will be the herald of a number of diseases known by names of the plants affected – geranium blackleg, pansy sickness, various crown rots, and so on. It is often caused by waterlogged ground. Destroy the affected plants and water the ground with one of the special compounds.

Many plants have specific diseases that affect their growth and cause wilting, bulb damage and rot. The gardener cannot know them all, but by keeping a keen eye on his flower beds and borders he shall spot the first sign of trouble, and be able to act quickly and efficiently.

Foxgloves and pyrethrum make a charming combination.

INDEX

ACKNOWLEDGEMENTS

The Publishers wish to thank the following for providing photographs in this book:
Eric Crichton 53, 82, 83, 84, 85, 86, 87, 88; The Garden Picture Library/Brian Carter 29; Insight Picture Library/Linda Burgess 31, 35; Andrew Lawson 56; Harry Smith Collection 60, 55b, 57.
The following photographs were taken specially for the Octopus Publishing Group Picture Library:
34, 51, 92; M Boys 2, 8t, 10, 11t, 11br, 22t, 33b, 38, 39b, 41t, 42t, 43tl & tr, 44, 45, 47t, c & bl, 62, 63l & r, 81, 93; Constance Spry & Cordon Bleu Group/Steve Lyne 28; W F Davidson 9 18, 22b, 23, 24, 46, 48, 79; J Harpur 6, 7, 8b, 11bl, 15, 17, 19, 21, 25, 33t, 36, 39t, 41b, 45, 47br, 55t, 64, 68, 72, 75, 77, 78, 90; N Holmes 42b, 65, 66; A Martin 54; G Wright 9, 14, 22c, 27, 32, 43b, 49, 61, 67, 69, 70, 74, 76, 80, 89.
Illustrations by Jim Robins.